D1028097

Managing Others
Creatively

Managing Creatively
a Very Practical Guide in Two Volumes

Volume 2

Managing Others
Creatively

by Ted Pollock, Ph.D.

Illustrations by
Ray Lewis

HAWTHORN BOOKS, INC.
Publishers / NEW YORK

Contents

Managing Others
Creatively

Chapter One

How Well Do You Handle People?

Ask any top executive to pinpoint the one personal characteristic most needed by a manager and the odds are overwhelmingly in favor of his answering, "The ability to work with people."

Why all the fuss over this single skill?

"Surely," you may say, "a successful executive does a lot more than just manage people. What about production, research and development, long-range planning, engineering, design, traffic and all the other concerns of a modern corporation?"

Consider these facts:

Executive decisions are carried out by—*people.*

By far, the largest single item in any operating budget is —*people.*

Most planning centers around the needs and abilities of— *people.*

The biggest, most valuable asset any company has is its— *people.*

By actual measurement, the average executive spends three-quarters of his working day dealing with—*people.*

A. H. Smith, former president of the New York Central Railroad, once defined his industry this way: "A railroad is 95 percent men and 5 percent iron." No modern executive, regardless of his industry, would disagree.

That's the reason for all the fuss. And for this book.

How well do *you* handle people? Do you take them for granted . . . or recognize the unique contribution of each to your department or business? Do you inspire them . . . or intimidate them? Do they feel like valued members of a team . . . or more like "hired hands"?

The answers you give to the following questions should provide you with a comprehensive profile of your "people-handling" capability.

1. When interviewing a potential employee, do you take whatever measures may be necessary to assure that you both have uninterrupted privacy for the duration of your meeting?

2. Do you, via a review of his application and résumé, brief yourself on his past experience, education, salary requirements, and so on, before sitting down with him?

3. Do you strive for an informal atmosphere in your interviews in order to put the applicant at his ease?

4. Are your questions open-ended, giving the interviewee an opportunity to speak at length, rather than "yes-or-no" oriented?

5. Are you ever guilty of hiring overqualified people, thus virtually guaranteeing their swift turnover due to boredom and lack of challenge?

6. Do you maintain your objectivity during an interview, ignoring such aspects of the applicant as his physical appearance, mode of dress, accent and the like (unless they are related to the work he will be doing) and sticking strictly to an evaluation of his skills?

7. Do you ever give your subordinates a chance to do something that will "upgrade" them—that is, something that will prepare them for "the next step up"?

8. Have you ever recommended one of your people for advancement, or transfer, even though it meant losing an exceptional man in your own department?

9. When was the last time you invited a subordinate to discuss with you in private any beefs he might have?

10. Name the weakest man on your "team." What have you done lately to help him improve?

11. Honestly, now—have you ever played favorites?

12. How would you rate morale among your people—excellent, good or just so-so?

13. If your answer is less than excellent, what can you do about it?

14. Are you ever guilty of criticizing a subordinate in front of a third party (including raising of voice if your office is not sound-proof)?

15. Do you wait until you have all the facts in a particular situation before criticizing any particular subordinate?

16. Do you ever lose your temper with the people under you?

17. Do you try to preface your criticism with some honest praise?

18. Do you ever use sarcasm when criticizing another?

19. Is your criticism generally constructive in nature?

20. Do you avoid discussing personalities when you criticize?

21. Do you try to remain obective while criticizing—that is, do you avoid jumping to conclusions about who is at fault and concentrate on *what* went wrong?

22. Are you ever guilty of assuming that because *you* know something, your people ought to know it, too?

23. Do you keep your instructions positive?

24. When giving complicated instructions, do you take pains to give them in some sort of logical sequence (*e.g.*, chronological order or simple to complex)?

25. When you explain something new to a subordinate, do you attempt to draw analogies with something he already knows rather than hitting him with something completely alien to his experience?

26. When possible, do you demonstrate what you mean—or use samples, charts, models, cutaways and so on?

27. Do you ask questions—and encourage questions from him—in the course of explaining something new to an employee?

28. Having given him your instructions and put him to work, do you check on his progress from time to time, without breathing down his neck?

29. Do your people really feel they can admit they don't understand what you want them to do without incurring your wrath?

30. Are your people afraid that stating a grievance will antagonize you?

31. When your subordinates are getting something off their chests, do you truly listen to them?

32. After hearing out a gripe that sounds valid, do you try to offer genuine redress? That is, do you tell the complainer, honestly and concretely, *what* you propose to do to remedy the situation—and *when* and *how?*

33. Do you ever express an opinion on the merits of a complaint or grievance before the pertinent facts have been uncovered and weighed?

34. If the complaint is invalid, do you take the trouble to explain calmly why?

35. When you have gotten to the root of a gripe and have taken care of it, do you explain to the employee what you have done and ask him if he finds your action or solution acceptable?

36. Do you ever try to motivate your people by appealing to their self-interest—that is, by showing them how they can also serve themselves in some way by doing what you want them to do (*e.g.,* how a certain procedure will save them time, avoid errors, or make their work easier)?

37. Do you try to introduce some *healthy* competition among subordinates—not the kind that leads to bitterness, but the kind that keeps them all on their toes?

38. Can you say, "no" to an employee without arousing anger in him?

39. Are you ever guilty of implying, by word or deed, that a subordinate is stupid?

40. Do you yourself set a good example for your people—by putting in a full day's work, pitching in on a big job when it is not strictly in your area, by assuming the responsibility for your decisions and your mistakes?

41. You've been emphatic about your position on a certain matter—a position with which a subordinate disagrees. It later turns out that you were dead wrong. What do you do? Bluster your way through? Let him know that he'd better not talk about it? Admit you were wrong?

42. On the other hand, suppose you are proven right. Do you gloat over your "victory"? Explain what *his* error was? Let the whole matter drop?

43. Are you generally courteous toward your people?

44. Before you reach any decisions affecting your employees, do you take into consideration their problems, aspirations, ambitions?

45. Would you say that the people who work under you consider you receptive to new ideas?

46. Do you see to it that they are kept informed on new developments, new policies, and the like that might affect them, on the job or off?

47. When possible, do you give them a chance to take part in decisions?

48. Do you show respect for your employees' knowledge—and, on occasion, defer to their expertise, even when you don't entirely agree with them?

49. Are you grooming someone to take your place?

50. Do you keep him informed of your plans and their progress?

51. Is he given practice in the fine art of thinking for himself?

52. Are you adding to his responsibilities, as well as to his authority, and giving him an opportunity to acquire all the skills he will need when the time comes for him to step into your shoes?

53. Do you give your people *reasonable* deadlines in which to get their work done?

54. Are you a "glory hog"—or when credit or compliments come your way, do you pass them on down to your staff?

55. Do you try to put each man "in business for himself" by assigning specific responsibilities for specific results?

56. Do you take the time to explain the *why* behind individual assignments?

57. Have you ever viewed a subordinate as a competitor?

58. Do you broaden your people's responsibilities as much as their performance merits?

59. Do you give your people *enough* to do (too little work, like too much, can wreck morale)?

60. Do you *practice* showing respect for the individual, no matter what his job or status?

61. Do you have a sense of humor on the job? Can you see the funny side of a set-back . . . a criticism . . . an error?

62. Do you let each person know, periodically, how he is getting along?

63. What have you done lately to make your people proud of the work they do?

64. Do your people know that you are ready and willing to take the responsibility for them? That, if necessary, you will go to bat for them?

65. Do you dominate your people to the point of eliminating initiative?

66. Are you aware that, as important as it may be, pay is by no means the only reward for which people work?

67. If you are aware of that fact, what other rewards do you offer your subordinates in their work?

68. Do you ask your people for advice in those areas in which they may have something to contribute?

69. Have you taught your people to tackle a difficulty by asking, "What's the problem?" rather than stating, "We're in trouble"?

70. Do they understand that the problem should be stated specifically in order to be solved intelligently—for example, "We have a production problem" is wrong,

whereas "We must boost production by at least eight percent" is correct?

71. Do they know where to get specific help for specific problems in your company?

72. Do you encourage them to stick with problems no matter how tough they are—and to look for new approaches?

73. Have you made it clear that you don't expect every problem to be solved overnight?

74. Do you stay out of their hair so that they have to solve the problem themselves—and come to you only when they've tried everything else?

75. Have you delegated some of your responsibilities downward, thus freeing yourself for more important work while encouraging growth among your subordinates?

76. At the same time, have you conferred authority commensurate with the added responsibility that you have delegated?

77. Have you given your people the feeling that they will assume new responsibilities as quickly as they prove themselves worthy of them?

78. Do you stand behind your subordinates' decisions once they have set upon a course of action in a given situation?

79. Do you display understanding for personal problems that may be besetting employees (e.g., permitting days off to settle pressing personal affairs)?

80. Do you periodically let employees know how they are doing, where they excel, where improvements can be made?

81. If you do practice this policy, are you able to discuss their status openly, without embarrassment or awkwardness?

82. Would you say that your subordinates admire you? If so, in what way (professionally, personally, etc.)?

83. Looking back over your career in management, would you say that you have helped more than your share of younger people get ahead?

84. Have any former subordinates of yours gone on to bigger and better things?
85. In view of the answers you have given to the previous questions, would *you* hire yourself as an executive if you applied for the job?

There, in an interrogative nutshell, you have the subjects to be dealt with at length in the following chapters.

We begin where all books should begin—at the beginning, with the first of your responsibilities as an executive: hiring the people you will be managing. And since the reverse side of the coin is firing, we briefly examine the techniques of that unhappy task.

The hiring process is, perhaps above all else, a specialized form of communication. So we turn our attention to several aspects of that important function: selling your ideas to others, instructing your people and, when necessary, criticizing them.

We then consider the general area of motivation, including an examination of what makes people tick, how to whip up employee enthusiasm, win cooperation, and improve morale.

But there never was, never will be, a large group of people working together that didn't experience its share of frictions and misunderstandings. Complaints and "people problems," therefore, engage our attention next.

Happily, if problem employees are inevitable, so are the other kind: dedicated, loyal, self-motivating, hard-working, talented people who deserve encouragement, recognition, and advancement. Spotting—and keeping—them are not only vital management responsibilities, but triple-A investments in your own future, for such high-potential people free you for bigger and better jobs. By the time you finish the last chapter, you should be equipped to begin to realize your own highest potential.

At that point, you should no longer need this book, having outgrown it; if you haven't, there is absolutely no penalty for rereading it.

Chapter Two

Hiring and Firing

When you consider the investment in terms of money, time, space, and training that an employee represents, it isn't difficult to understand why the ability to interview job applicants effectively can be a highly valuable asset in a manager. It not only enables him to hire the best qualified people for his own department, thereby making his own job easier, but it also gives him a rare opportunity to make an important and enduring contribution to his company's overall productivity and cost effectiveness.

Because employment interviewing brings two people together, with all the unique traits and idiosyncrasies that make them individuals, its successful conduct is far more likely to be an art than a science.

You, the interviewer, must feel your way throughout the interview, "reading between the lines," pursuing some things further than others, sometimes intuiting what is left unsaid—and why. It can be a delicate and challenging assignment.

Nevertheless, there are some useful techniques to bear in mind as you talk to any potential employee.

PUT HIM AT EASE

This would seem only elementary common sense, but many managers ignore the importance of establishing a friendly atmosphere in their interviews. They let the applicant cool his heels in an impersonal waiting room, then permit all kinds of interruptions to interfere with their conversation once the man is in their office. They play the role of "big shot executive" to the hilt, avoid any sign of interest in the applicant as a human being and finish the interview with an ego-crushing dismissal.

Yet, all it really takes to put a man at his ease is some fundamental good manners and common sense.

If, for example, you have made an appointment with him for 9:30, make sure that you are prepared to see him at 9:30, not 9:45 or 10:00. Admittedly, sometimes the unexpected does occur and you cannot keep an appointment, but *as a general rule, be punctual.*

Never be ignorant of the man's background when you see him. It is discomfiting and somewhat humiliating to have to sit quietly in an alien environment while the interviewer slowly goes over your application, rustling papers and, perhaps, occasionally lifting an eyebrow. Make it your business to see the application form well in advance of the personal interview so that you need only refer to it occasionally during the meeting.

Keep it private, too. Looking for a job is seldom a pleasant experience, and an interviewer who takes telephone calls or allows his secretary or visitors to interrupt the session at will is really saying that he does not consider the interview very important. It doesn't require much imagination or sensitivity to figure out what the applicant's feelings must be under such circumstances.

An air of informality can help an interview by setting the applicant at his ease. Try eliminating the desk that usually stands between the interviewer and interviewee, either by sitting in a chair facing the applicant or by meeting across a table in a conference room. It's a subtle touch, but one worth considering. For by doing away with the "official" air of an office, you encourage man-to-man communications and increase the chances of a frank exchange of information.

Finally, be friendly. You need not overwhelm the man with curiosity over his personal life or simulate a warmth which you do not truly feel. But a business interview need not be *solely* business. A few introductory pleasantries or a sincere question about the applicant's children may be enough to establish the climate you are seeking.

In short, be human.

KNOW WHAT YOU'RE TALKING ABOUT

If it is true that you are talking to a man in order to learn about him when you conduct an interview, it is equally true that he is there to learn about you, your department and your company.

You therefore owe him certain information and in order to live up fully to this responsibility, you must be completely familiar with, and up-to-date on, such areas of information as your company's policies . . . benefits program . . . what it expects from its employees . . . its training facilities . . . and so on.

Part of your job, remember, is to do some low-pressure selling of your firm to the prospective employee. There is sometimes a temptation to overdo this by exaggerating opportunities, pay scales or benefits. But if you cannot impress the interviewee by sticking to the facts, you are far better off finding that out during the interview period than after hiring him, when mounting disappointments will sour him on his job, on you, and on the company.

Give him as accurate a picture as possible, therefore, of the work he will be doing in this job, the people with whom he will be most in contact, his work location and hours. If possible, show him where he will work. If he will occasionally (or frequently) be asked to put in overtime, work on weekends or change shifts, tell him so. It is obviously not only basic honesty; it is also self-protection for you, should he be hired and later complain about working conditions.

Clearly, there is little to be gained in the long run from the misrepresentation of a job, its responsibilities or requirements. Nor should you make promises that you cannot possibly keep. Fundamental to effective man-manager relations is mutual trust based on mutual honesty. You will get neither if you do not give them first. And the interview, being your initial confrontation with an employee, is the place to begin.

Stick to the facts. Tell the truth. Don't make promises you cannot keep.

CONTROL THE INTERVIEW

Controlling an interview does not mean that you must run it like some Grand Inquisitor while the interviewee meekly answers your questions from under a blinding spotlight. Rather, it is to suggest that you structure and conduct the interview to serve your own interests—that is, to determine whether the applicant is the best person for the job that is available.

The skill most required here is skill in asking questions.

Your questions, of course, should make the applicant think and respond in some detail. So avoid questions that can be answered by a simple "yes" or "no." You will learn little from them. Instead, ask open-ended questions that encourage the interviewee to answer in some depth and detail: "Do you consider your progress on your present job representative of your ability? Why?" "What would you say were your chief responsibilities in your last job?" "In your opinion, what are your strongest points?"

Avoid questions which in any way carry a suggestion of the answer you are seeking, like, "You enjoy solitary work, don't you?" "I imagine you left Consolidated for more money?" "What's your experience been in doing business with that double-dealing Acme Company?" If you persist in asking such questions, you will only hear what you want or expect to hear, not necessarily what the interviewee truly believes.

Your questions should elicit answers on such general subjects as how the applicant feels about his current job, his atti-

tudes toward people, his job objectives and his own assessment
of himself as a worker and human being.

BE OBJECTIVE

With the best of intentions, an interviewer can be prejudiced—
for a pretty girl, for example, or *against* a man who reminds him
of his father-in-law.

Lack of objectivity can sometimes be very subtle. For instance, many of us are unconsciously thrown off the track by
what might be termed the "halo effect"—a tendency to allow
our overall judgment to be influenced by certain individual
characteristics. Example: if a man speaks well, we conclude
that he will work well, too; or we assume that a person who
looks you squarely in the eye when he speaks is honest.

Some of us tend to overgeneralize as well. Just because a
person behaves in a certain way in one situation, we conclude
that he will automatically behave in the same way in all situations. Example: a man defends an unpopular point of view; we
infer that he is an independent thinker on all subjects.

Finally, interviewers occasionally fall into the trap of habitually seeking overqualified applicants. They will only hire
those people whose experience and knowledge far surpass the
requirements of a job. The eventual outcome is a foregone conclusion—overqualified people holding jobs which they find boring, without challenge and unrewarding. Such employees don't
remain on a job very long. Before the interviewer knows it, he
is going through the entire process all over again—and is
doomed to repeat his error *ad infinitum.*

Make it your business to know what the job requires in
the way of knowledge, skill, and experience and look for people who meet—but don't vastly surpass—the qualifications for
the job.

It's mutual job satisfaction insurance.

BEWARE OF THESE DANGER SIGNALS

There are certain questions to which you should receive satisfactory answers. If you do not, you may legitimately decide that a "reasonable doubt" exists as to the wisdom of hiring the applicant.

For example, be wary of applicants—

WHO CANNOT GIVE GOOD REASONS FOR LEAVING PREVIOUS JOBS. If they cannot talk about it, perhaps there was something unspeakable about their departure.

WHOSE EARNINGS HAVE BEEN SUBSTANTIALLY HIGHER THAN THE AMOUNT THEY ARE NOW WILLING TO ACCEPT. Think. Why?

WHO HAVE HAD FIVE OR MORE JOBS IN THE LAST FIVE YEARS. It is highly unlikely that all that moving was strictly voluntary.

WHO HAVE DOMESTIC DIFFICULTIES. At best, personal problems eventually impair job performance; at worst, they may be indicative of personality problems that can adversely affect the work of others as well.

WHO HAVE DEBTS GREATER THAN CAN BE REPAID WITHIN TWO YEARS OUT OF NORMAL INCOME. They may be either considering "moving on," thus representing a bad investment on your part, or—in desperation—doing something foolish that you will both regret.

The job interview should be the beginning of a good working relationship between employee and manager. When it is, the manager-interviewer may rightly take credit for having shown good judgment. But when it isn't, he must also take the blame. You can stack the odds in favor of taking bows instead of brickbats by following the suggestions discussed here.

But let's face it. Despite your best efforts, once in a while an employee simply does not work out. When that's the case, what do you do?

Given the choice, the average executive would almost certainly prefer to walk over broken glass barefooted than discharge an employee.

Perhaps it's the traditional American bias on behalf of the underdog. Maybe, deep down, an executive feels responsible for, and guilty about, such a situation developing at all; he either hired the man in the first place or apparently failed in "bringing him along" at an acceptable pace; either way, it reflects upon his judgment and skill. Or, possibly, it is a natural reluctance born of empathy—"That poor guy could be me!"

Firing a man is a tough, thankless job, certainly. It can create unpleasantness, affect morale, and prey on the executive's mind until he becomes ineffective on the job himself. Some firms, recognizing the problem, actually hire outside specialists to do their firing for them. These consultants have devised an assortment of ingenious techniques to ease a man out of his job almost without his realizing it. They have even invented a variety of euphemisms, like "dehiring" and "outplacement," to describe what they do.

And yet, there are cases where firing a man face-to-face is the only way out. A worker may be an expensive incompetent, a disrupting influence in his department, the cause of major blunders. For the sake of everyone concerned, including himself, he is best discharged.

So—what *do* you do?

A better starting point, perhaps, is to consider what you *don't* do.

SOME PRECAUTIONS

No matter what the provocation, the executive who fires any employee on the spur of the moment is very apt to regret doing so later. The complicated employer-employee relations laws of today, plus some plain good business reasons, make it advisable to exercise maximum care in any employee dismissal. Here are some guidelines.

BE SURE THAT NO LABOR CONTRACT IS VIOLATED, if such exists, for overlooking some small point in such an agreement can be very costly. Check and double check each specific case before taking action.

MAKE CERTAIN OF THE LAW OF THE STATE in which business is being transacted. It never pays to guess about or rely upon old knowledge of such law, even though your firm has done business in the state for many years. It is equally hazardous to assume that the labor laws of one's own state apply in another when operations cross such lines.

NEVER, BUT NEVER, FIRE AN EMPLOYEE IN A STATE OF ANGER or high emotion. Under these circumstances even the best of us is likely to say things that will be regretted later.

BE SURE YOU MAY NOT WANT TO REHIRE the employee in the future. Because you no longer have need of an individual's particular talents today is no guarantee that the situation will not change in the future. It always helps to preserve as pleasant a situation as possible in any dismissal action so that the individual can be available at some time in the future when he or she may be needed.

With these words of warning out of the way, let's assume that someone who works under you has to be fired. It may be due to economic necessity, a basic change in corporate strategy or a simple case of incompetency.

Whatever the reason, there you are, faced by the necessity of telling somebody that his services are no longer required. How do you do it? Some suggestions:

BE PREPARED

Firing someone is uncomfortable enough a situation without adding to the discomfort by hemming and hawing. Before talking to the employee, know what you will say—the solid, indisputable reasons for letting him go.

If it is a question of retrenchment, have the figures at your fingertips.

If there has been a shift in company planning (*e.g.*, due to the loss of one or more large orders, a merger, the phasing out of a product line), explain as clearly as you can the repercussions as they affect your manpower needs.

If it is a question of the employee's personal ability or lack of it, be ready to cite chapter and verse.

Part of your preparation will have to be an anticipation of possible counterarguments and excuses the employee will bring up. He may try to rationalize a poor performance by blaming his tools, his supervisor, his fellow workers—anyone or anything but himself. A factual summary of his job performance from date of hiring, with references to specific events, can go a long way toward winning his agreement, however reluctant, with your decision.

You owe it to the employee to let him know the real reason for his dismissal. Do *not* vaguely slough it off on the "front office" or "general business conditions." Rather, tell him as explicitly as you can *why* you are compelled to let him go.

BE CONSIDERATE

At the same time, remember that getting fired is a terrific blow to the ego. If it's the truth, explain that it is not the calibre of the employee's work that is at fault.

If it *is* a question of his performance, there are ways of saying so that leave a minimum residue of bad feeling:

"You're an extremely well-qualified draftsman, but a little

too weak in practical engineering experience for the position, Jack."

"When you first came here, we agreed that the position required someone with more background. You've done pretty well for someone with limited experience, but the work is too important to risk any more wrong decisions."

Try to find *something* in his performance to commend before you point out his failing.

One observation: don't criticize anything about his character or competence that he can't do anything about. It is, for example, of absolutely no help to a man to be told that his inability to get along with others is absolutely infuriating. That's the way he is and he will probably never change.

DO IT IN PRIVATE

As self-evident as this may seem, there are some managers who will unfeelingly announce a firing in front of the employee's fellow workers. Not only is this in poor taste; it will invariably sour those remaining, who may wonder when they will feel the guillotine blade.

It's far better to invite the employee into your office and close the door, making whatever arrangements may be necessary in order not to be disturbed.

While there is certainly no good time to fire anyone, the end of a work day is preferable to the beginning and the last day of the work week to the first. Dismissal is a shock, remember, and a man is better off if he doesn't have to face his colleagues immediately after such a trauma. With a weekend to mull things over, adjust to the situation and, perhaps, make tentative plans for his future, he is in better psychological shape to face his fellow workers and the world in general.

BE BUSINESSLIKE

While a dismissal strikes at the roots of a man's self-esteem and you should, of course, be considerate of his feelings, you are headed for trouble if you allow yourself to get too involved with his personal problems in the process.

The rule: be considerate, of course, but be businesslike too.

The two are not mutually exclusive. Give him the facts as objectively as you can, explain clearly the problems involved in his work, but avoid any attempts at personality analysis or lay psychiatry. Certainly, steer clear of any character denigration.

Depending on the rank and seniority of the man being fired and any special consideration that may pertain, your interview will vary in length. But it is best for all concerned that it be kept brief—5–15 minutes. Longer sessions tend to go around in circles and little is gained in the process. Don't prolong the agony.

BE HELPFUL

If the employee is entitled to severance pay, accumulated vacation time, or other remuneration, let him know exactly what he may expect by way of "final settlement." If you can, help him relocate or offer letters of recommendation. If you can suggest ways in which he can improve as a worker (*e.g.,* going back to school), by all means do so.

The important thing to bear in mind is that you are dealing with a human being, with the same general goals in life and sensitivities as you. A little empathy will go a long way toward making the ordeal of firing more palatable to both of you.

Chapter Three

Put Your Ideas Across Effectively!

The children of a prominent Bostonian once decided to give him a novel gift for his birthday—a book on the family's history.

They hired an experienced biographer, but felt honor-bound to warn him of one problem: Uncle Charles, who had gone to the electric chair for murder. They couldn't ignore his existence, but they certainly didn't want to publicize his shame.

Fortunately, the biographer was a professional.

"No problem," he reassured them. "I'll just say that Uncle Charles occupied the chair of applied electronics at one of our leading governmental institutions. He was attached to his position by the strongest of ties. And his sudden death came as a great shock."

Moral: you can do almost anything you care to do with language, including confusing the issue and hiding the truth.

Yet, as an executive, in a typical work day, you doubtlessly participate in some, or all, of the following activities: you issue instructions; clarify policies; write letters, memos and reports; address committees; talk to employees, colleagues, salesmen, and customers. A good part of your day is spent in explaining, describing, persuading, asking, and answering. In short, you spend a lot of time dealing with people through words. Use those words poorly, incorrectly or ambiguously and you can cause a great deal of mischief.

But learn to put your ideas across effectively and you will:

1. GET THINGS DONE WITH DISPATCH because others will understand what you want—the very first time.
2. SAVE TIME by avoiding errors, misunderstandings, and needless backtracking.
3. WIN COOPERATION FROM PEOPLE by successfully "selling" them on your ideas.
4. BECOME A CLEARER THINKER because thinking is communication, too—with yourself.

Here is a simple program for putting your ideas across effectively every single time.

KNOW WHAT YOU WANT TO SAY

Incredible as it may sound, many people are poor communicators simply because they do not take the time or make the effort to get their ideas straight in their own minds. They settle for a vague or fuzzy *shadow* of an idea, then grow angry when they fail to get it across to others.

Fortunately, there is a virtually fool-proof way to pretest any idea for clarity: *try writing it out.*

There isn't an idea in the world that cannot be expressed on paper, from "1 + 1 = 2" to "All men are created equal." By the same token, if it *cannot* be written out, it isn't a completely developed idea. The very act of finding the appropriate words with which to express it compels you to think it through.

MAKE SURE IT'S CLEAR

Okay. *You* know what you want to say. Now you are ready to "send" your message on one of the most perilous of journeys— from your mind to that of another human being—making sure that nothing is lost, or gained, along the way.

Here are four techniques for doing just that.

TALK THE OTHER FELLOW'S LANGUAGE

In every field, from advertising to zoology, there has developed a special vocabulary fully understood by those in it. But should a zoologist find himself talking to a lawyer, he would take pains to phrase his thoughts in nontechnical language.

The same is true of all of us. No matter how we earn our living, on the job we talk a special language. Those with whom we work readily understand what we say. But others—even those in different departments of the same company—often don't. We have to "translate" our thoughts for them.

Executives in particular tend to forget this when dealing with the "outside world." A manager of a metals plant, for example, may *think* he's talking Basic English when he says, "This alloy covers steel with a protective film of chromium oxide," but it's gibberish to most people. What he *ought* to say to a nontechnical audience is something like, "This mixture of metals, applied to steel, protects it against corrosion from the water vapor and natural salts in air."

So unless you *know* that your audience understands the jargon of your trade, business, or profession, keep your message simple.

BE CONCRETE

It's always easier to visualize specific *things* and solid facts than vague generalities. Take advantage of this whenever you have an idea to put across. Tell your listener or correspondent in specific terms exactly what's on your mind. Paint word-pictures. Form images that he can readily see, grasp and understand.

Don't say, "In a few weeks." Say, "In three weeks."

Don't say, "Delay can be costly." Say, "Delay will cost us $640."

Don't say, "I heard that. . . ." Say, "Jack Brewster told me. . . ."

Don't say, "You'll save money." Say, "You'll save $50 a week."

Be concrete.

BE A SHOWMAN

When Joseph E. Levine, the movie mogul, first launched his career with the release of the film, *Hercules,* he wanted to impress the public with the fact that he was spending a million dollars to promote it.

Mr. Levine could have issued a publicity release to announce the fact. But he didn't. He could have held a press conference and made the announcement there. But he didn't. Instead, he hosted a formal party for the press at one of New York's most prestigious hotels and there, on a table, protected by armed guards, lay $1 million *in cash,* for all to see. The party made headlines, of course—the kind of advertising no money could ever buy.

He got his message across—with a bang.

You will, too, if you take the trouble to dramatize your message.

How? By appealing to more than one of your audience's senses. Tell him (them) your idea, by all means, but don't stop there. *Demonstrate* it. Draw a picture. Show him a graph. Point to a model. Hold up a chart. Hand him a photograph. Strike a gong if necessary.

In short, bring a touch of P. T. Barnum to your communication. It's sure-fire.

USE YOUR VOICE

Read the following seven sentences aloud, emphasizing in each case the italicized word. (The various meanings given by your vocal inflections are included parenthetically.)

I didn't tell John you were stupid.   (Someone else told him.)

I *didn't* tell John you were stupid.   (I'm keeping the fact a secret.)

I didn't *tell* John you were stupid.	(I only hinted at it.)
I didn't tell *John* you were stupid.	(I told everyone *but* John.)
I didn't tell John *you* were stupid.	(I said that someone around here was stupid. He must have figured out it was you by himself.)
I didn't tell John you *were* stupid.	(I told him you *are* stupid.)
I didn't tell John you were *stupid.*	(I merely voiced my conviction that you weren't very smart.)

Quite a difference in implied meanings, isn't there? And what is true of this simple sentence is true of almost everything we say. *How* we voice our thoughts can make the difference between getting an idea across . . . and disaster.

If your message is intended to whip up enthusiasm, inject enthusiasm into your voice. If you wish to stress the importance of what you are saying, "put italics" under your words. Monotony breeds boredom, so use vocal ups and downs to keep your listener attentive.

HIGHLIGHT THE BENEFITS

Look at a group photograph. Where do your eyes dart first? To yourself.

Go to sleep and have a dream. Who is usually the central character? Yourself.

Open a newspaper and turn to the stock market quotations. What is your main concern? The status of *your* stocks.

To a large extent, we are all self-centered. That's not a criticism—merely a fact. Nature has made us that way in order to perpetuate our species. From time to time, especially in crises, we can overcome this human trait and sacrifice our own interests for others, but in the ordinary course of events, we are inescapably "self-oriented." We respond most animatedly to those things that affect our comfort, happiness, safety and finances.

Take advantage of this fact in your communications. Whenever possible, phrase your message in "what's-in-it-for-me" terms, for that is the unspoken question uppermost in your listener's mind.

Don't ask a man to accept your idea for what it *is;* ask him to accept it for what it will *do* for him.

Want your boss to okay a new billing machine? Don't describe the operation of a slick, new gadget. Do explain how it will eliminate errors, speed up invoicing, boost profits.

Want an employee to use his safety equipment? Don't tell him what an injured worker costs your firm. Do describe the injuries he may sustain if he continues his neglect.

Take the very next idea you have and, bearing in mind who your listener will be, express it in terms of the benefits he stands to gain from it—and watch your powers of persuasion grow!

BE ENTHUSIASTIC

"When you're introducing a new product to a buyer," the sales manager for a famous perfume company once explained, "it's not enough simply to have a story to tell. You must tell it with fire. Before he even takes an item out of its case, our salesman will confide, 'Do I have something for you!' While opening the case, he'll say, 'This perfume is like nothing you've ever handled before.' Up goes the lid. 'Why, it's been jamming counters from Seattle to Philly.' Down goes the lid. 'Jones in Cleveland sold 10 dozen the very first week.'

"By the time the buyer smells the perfume, he's genuinely excited. Then it's relatively easy to get him to sign an initial order for half a gross."

That's the magic of enthusiasm. It triggers curiosity. It stimulates interest. It arouses desire. It's contagious.

But a word of caution: don't oversell.

Although a judicious amount of enthusiasm can help you

put your idea across, beware the all-too-human tendency to announce, "This is the greatest idea you've ever heard!"

By overestimating the advantages of your brainstorm, you may inadvertently sour your listener on your notion even before he's heard you out. He may think, "Okay, big shot—I *dare* you to convince me." There is also the possibility that your idea is *not* perfect. You'll feel very foolish if, after listening to you, the other fellow immediately points out why it's a downright poor idea.

Further, should your idea prove only moderately successful, it may be considered a flop simply because it did not live up to your overly optimistic predictions. Any future ideas you present will find tough sledding.

The word: undersell. It is not incompatible with enthusiasm.

ANTICIPATE OBJECTIONS

Ideas are almost always suspect. People dislike having to change their views or actions. They much prefer to let things go along as they have, for the *status quo* is familiar and comfortable—a known quantity. It takes energy and thought and concentration to learn something new and people are naturally a bit lazy.

As the originator of an idea, you automatically become a threat to "Things-As-They-Are" as well as to the people who are committed to them.

Their reaction to your idea is predictable: suspicion. Sometimes, this suspicion takes the form of lack of attention to what you are saying. Sometimes, it manifests itself in heated argument. Most often, it assumes the guise of objections—one or more reasons for not accepting the change you are advocating: "It's too impractical." "We've always done it this way." "Too risky."

Of course, these objections may not necessarily be rationalizations. They may be valid. No matter which they are, however, you can largely neutralize them by anticipating them.

How can you anticipate the objections apt to be raised against your idea? By consciously and diligently examining it for flaws beforehand.

Does it require too much money? Time? Personnel? Does it depend on any unproven assumptions? Has something similar to it failed in the past? Is there *any* good reason why it shouldn't work?

By asking, and answering, pointed questions like these yourself, *before* you make your idea public, you can probe it for weaknesses, modify it accordingly and strengthen it until it is virtually "objection-proof."

Some examples:

"Even though the initial cost will be $1500 more than we budgeted for such a job, these figures *prove* that we'll save more in the long run."

"It's the easiest machine of its kind to operate and turns out more copies per minute than any other on the market, even though it is a little larger than most."

"True—we won't see any profit from the new operation for four or five years, but by 1980, when it's in full swing, it will be responsible for 30 percent of our production and 35 percent of our profit."

By bringing up the objection to your idea yourself—and disposing of it convincingly—you disarm your listener with reasons for ignoring or discounting the reservations that would normally occur to him.

He almost can't help but agree with you.

USE THE TECHNIQUES FOR SELLING CHANGE

Since most new ideas will require that your people accept some kind of change in their environments, the *kind* of change you want to institute will often determine the method you use to "sell" it to your people. But you should find the following observations, proven by carefully controlled experimentation, helpful. Researchers into the subject have discovered that:

1. CHANGE IS MORE ACCEPTABLE WHEN IT IS UNDERSTOOD

Few things can trigger rumors, resentment, and recalcitrance more quickly than a change that is not explained. Such an approach smacks of corporate callousness to personal feelings and appears to reinforce the notion that the company views its employees as faceless cogs in an all-important mechanism. A clear explanation of *why* the change is being instituted (*e.g.*, to eliminate costly procedures, make a department more efficient, remove a safety hazard) can put rumors to rest, raise morale, avoid misunderstandings.

2. CHANGE IS MORE ACCEPTABLE WHEN IT DOES NOT THREATEN SECURITY

Prove that the change will not adversely affect a man's income or future and you will have gone a long way toward winning his approval of it.

3. CHANGE IS MORE ACCEPTABLE WHEN THE PEOPLE AFFECTED BY IT HAVE HELPED TO CREATE IT

The classic study of this phenomenon was conducted in a clothing factory in the 1940's. Two researchers worked with four groups of factory operators who were paid on a modified piece-rate basis. A minor change in the work procedure of each group was introduced in a different way to see what kinds of resistance to change would develop.

The change was introduced to Group 1 by what was called a "no-participation" method. Some staff people called Group 1 into a room, announced that there was a need for minor change in their methods, then explained the change and the reason for it. The group was sent back to work with instructions to use the new method.

The work change was introduced to Group 2 through a "participation-through-representation" approach, which was a variation of the approach used with Groups 3 and 4.

These two groups, 3 and 4, were introduced to the change

on a "total participation" basis. The groups met with the staff, who demonstrated the need for cost reduction. The need for savings was accepted by all. Then the groups discussed how current work methods could be improved. When, after long discussion, new work methods were agreed upon, all the factory operators were trained in the new methods.

The follow-up study revealed that the most striking difference was between Group 1, the no-participation group, and Groups 3 and 4, the total-participation groups. The production of Group 1 dropped by one-third immediately and stayed there. In addition, resentment against the change was obvious, hostility toward management developed and there was a definite lack of cooperation with the supervisor. In the first 40 days after the change, 17 percent of the operators quit.

Groups 3 and 4 performed quite differently. After a slight initial drop in productivity, there was a rapid recovery and a leveling off at a higher productivity rate than before. There were no signs of hostility to management and no one quit during the term of the experiment.

The moral appears crystal clear: resistance to change can be overcome by getting the people who will be affected by it to participate in making it.

4. CHANGE IS MORE ACCEPTABLE IF IT HAS BEEN PLANNED

Prove to your people that a great deal of thought has preceded the change, with the alternatives to it carefully considered, and they will usually "buy" it.

5. CHANGE IS MORE ACCEPTABLE WHEN IT IS INAUGURATED AFTER PREVIOUS CHANGE HAS BEEN ASSIMILATED

In other words, for best results allow one change to be digested and accepted before introducing another.

IN A NUTSHELL

There you have them—five easy rules for putting your ideas across.

1. *Know what you want to say.*
2. *Make sure it's clear:*
    (a) *Talk the other fellow's language.*
    (b) *Be concrete.*
    (c) *Be a showman.*
    (d) *Use your voice.*
3. *Highlight the benefits.*
4. *Anticipate objections.*
5. *Use the techniques for selling change.*

Next time you are trying to persuade or sell someone, try these techniques and—*put your ideas across!*

Chapter Four

How to Give Instructions

Of all the communications skills that an executive needs to be more effective on the job, skill in giving instructions is almost certainly the most neglected.

Yet, consider how important it is. Employees require guidance and direction. Customers want information. Suppliers must be informed of your needs and desires. Laymen frequently need "translations" of technical jargon.

The worker who neglects to use his safety equipment . . . the irate customer who is having difficulty with your product . . . the confused supplier who ships you the wrong equipment —all may be the innocent victims of your garbled or misleading instructions in the first place.

You can avoid 95 percent of the misunderstandings that plague you and your business by mastering the basic principles of giving instructions. They aren't difficult. The few minutes it will take you to learn them and make them a part of your daily routine will be amply rewarded by the elimination of costly backtracking, elaborate explanations and lost time. Moreover, you will be able to pass them along to your subordinates.

Here is all it takes to give effective instructions.

GIVE THE "BIG PICTURE"

Since it is easier for a person to learn something when he understands a little about it than when it is entirely meaningless to him, you can dramatically increase that understanding by offering your student a bird's-eye view of the material you will be covering before you actually begin.

If you are instructing a group of people, you might pass out a one-page outline of what you will be covering. If you are speaking to an individual, you might synopsize in an informal way what you are about to tell him. By so doing, you not only prove that the "trip" is worthwhile; you also make it easier for him to accompany you.

When you can, therefore, sketch the "big picture" for your people before filling in the details.

START WITH THE KNOWN

Try to imagine a new shape, unlike anything you have ever seen before. Difficult? Impossible! You might come up with a strange-looking circle or an erratic combination of squares and triangles, but you cannot invent a brand new shape.

Why? Because we are inescapably the prisoners of what we already know.

Or, consider this example. You have never seen an automobile made of solid gold, have you? Yet, it is not particularly difficult to conjure up such an image, is it?

Why? Because you have seen automobiles and you have seen (or, at least, are familiar with the qualities of) gold. Your mind has no trouble in combining these two familiar objects in order to invent a new one.

People learn most easily when they begin with something they already know, then move on to the unfamiliar. What they know forms a solid foundation upon which they can build new concepts.

If you are trying to teach a youngster how to add, you don't tell him, "Two plus two equal four." The idea is too abstract; it has no reality for him. But tell him, "If you have two marbles and I give you two more marbles, you have four marbles," and you have gone a long way in bringing the mathematical concept of addition down to earth for him. Marbles are within his experience, as are apples, fingers, balls and ice cream cones. Only after he has grown accustomed to adding marbles, fingers, balls and ice cream cones can he eliminate them from his thinking and finally comprehend the far deeper concept of two plus two.

That is the basic idea behind the second rule for giving effective instructions: "Start with the known; introduce the unknown gradually."

If, for example, you wish to explain a new policy to your customers, you might phrase it this way: "It's like a cash discount (*the known*). Just as you earn a price reduction by paying cash for a purchase, from now on you will earn a two percent credit against future orders on all orders placed with us during July and August (*the unknown*)."

Or, suppose you wanted to institute a new procedure in your office. You might say, "Starting next month, we will handle all incoming bills as if they were our own outgoing invoices (*the known*). That is, they will be turned over to Gloria for checking against the original order, photostated and filed for quick reference (*the unknown*)."

Try it yourself. The very next time you must explain something, search for an analogy familiar to the person with whom you are communicating—and watch that bulb light up over his head!

START WITH THE SIMPLE

Just as the known paves the way for the unknown, so does the simple for the complex.

If you must issue complicated instructions, or an overwhelming number of them, remember the importance of introducing them gradually, starting with the most comprehensible, then leading to the more difficult.

There are two reasons why this approach works:

1. Start with the toughest part of your instructions and you run the risk of alienating your "student" at the very outset. Convinced that he'll never understand all you're going to say, he will promptly "tune out"—even though he may *look* attentive.
2. Since learning is based on memory, instructions presented in a memorable way stand the best chance of being learned. An easy way to make instructions memorable is to impose some kind of logic on them. And moving from the simple to the complex *is* one kind of logic.

Thus, if you want to explain a new delivery system to a supplier, you might put it this way:

"Beginning with your next shipment, make sure that all replacement parts are packed in boxes of 100 or multiples of 100 (*the simple*). These should be clearly identified by label or stencil and piled up on our receiving platform under the sign labeled, 'Replacement Parts.' All new parts should continue to be packed in gross lots and delivered as before (*the complex*)."

No matter what your instructions, no matter who your "students," you will be a more effective "teacher" if you move from the simple to the complex.

KEEP YOUR INSTRUCTIONS POSITIVE

The human brain is a delicate—and tricky—mechanism. It doesn't always listen the way we'd like it to. And it is far from infallible. Tell it *not* to do something and, in the process of sending the prohibition to the rest of your body, it may activate the very muscles that ought to be relaxed.

Anyone who has ever used a typewriter is familiar with this sort of mental short circuit. Type a word incorrectly and, as you are erasing it, you will think, "I mustn't repeat that error." No sooner do your fingers begin to move again than—lo and behold!—in five out of ten cases, you repeat the same error.

Thus, if you say, "Claire, don't send out invoices until the orders have been on the road for three days," it's even money that Claire's brain will erroneously associate orders on the road with instructions about sending out invoices. She'll "pull a blank" on the three-day restriction. It is far more effective to say, "Claire, send out the invoices three days after an order is on the road."

So, if you want to avoid errors and misunderstandings, keep your instructions positive.

DEMONSTRATE AND DRAMATIZE

The very existence of a major metropolitan newspaper is being threatened by a damaging rumor. The paper, it is whispered, is on the brink of extinction because it carries too much advertising, not enough news: readers are deserting it by the tens of thousands.

Even as the first cancellations arrive from advertisers, the editorial board is engaged in a series of emergency meetings. Obviously, something must be done—quickly.

But what?

The answer comes in an inspired flash of insight. The board decides to excerpt all the reading matter from just one regular edition of the newspaper—exclusive of advertisements—and publish it as a *book*. When the volume is printed, it contains no fewer than 300 pages. Copies are rushed to advertisers.

Black on white and between hard covers, that newspaper proves its point beyond a shadow of a doubt: it offers its readers *daily* as much news and features as would occupy the pages of a book costing several dollars. And it sells all this for pennies.

The rumor dies in its tracks.

Why? Because the editorial board knew that the swiftest way to get its message across was to dramatize it.

That's often true of giving instructions, too. By *showing* your listener something or *doing* something in front of him, you can frequently clarify what otherwise might require hours of talking. It is, for example, far easier to demonstrate the use of an adding machine than to verbalize over it.

By augmenting your spoken instructions with a demonstration, you help your student learn faster, too, for you appeal to more than just his sense of hearing. And the more of his senses you manage to engage in your lesson, the deeper the impression you are bound to make upon him.

Besides, everybody likes a "show." We enjoy watching things happen. And what we enjoy, we pay attention to. And remember.

Whenever you can, therefore, demonstrate and dramatize your instructions.

PROVIDE PRACTICE

What we *do* reinforces learning because it impresses not only our eyes and ears, but also establishes a "motor habit"—a certain pattern of behavior. By "learning with our muscles," we are really repeating to ourselves in an additional language the verbal lesson to which we have just been exposed. And repetition is one valid avenue of learning.

In your instructions, therefore, try to provide opportunities for the student to practice wherever possible. If you have been explaining how to write out a purchase order, for example, let him take a crack at writing out one himself. If you want him to master the techniques of working up a budget, give him a chance to work on one.

Practice may not *always* make perfect, but it sure helps.

ENCOURAGE QUESTIONS

One of the most costly assumptions made by people who habitually issue instructions to others is that the absence of questions signifies perfect understanding.

Not so. There may be no questions because your listener is

uninterested in what you are saying, or bored with your presentation, or timid, or daydreaming.

So encourage questions. Ask in a pleasant way whether you have made everything clear. And if there are still no questions, turn the tables on your student: ask *him* questions to make sure he fully understands your instructions. For example: "Smith, what are the two main danger signals to watch for on this machine?" "When will we be offering the new models?" "When is the best time to order supplies for the summer months?"

Don't make your questioning sound like an inquisition, of course, but be persistent. If your student cannot answer your questions satisfactorily, repeat your instructions and, if necessary, clarify them. It will pay off in better understanding.

KEEP TABS ON YOUR PROGRESS

You will never know just how well your instructions have "taken" unless you check on results regularly. Wait too long and you may be too late—error may have already taken its toll.

Keeping tabs on a man doesn't mean hovering over him all day and criticizing his every move. It does mean visiting him now and then and finding out whether he is having any difficulties with which you can help him. This can be a good time, too, to give him a pat on the back, if deserved. Everybody appreciates a compliment, so don't be miserly with your approval. If a man performs a new job well, tell him so. If he asks a relevant question, let him know. If he solves a difficult problem, congratulate him. You will not only boost his morale and self-confidence; you will encourage him to continue the good work.

Chapter Five

"The Trouble with You Is . . . "

If you have already found Shangri-La and work alongside its perfect creatures, you have no need to criticize others. Nobody under you ever goofs. Instructions are followed to the letter and with dispatch. Your employees work at peak efficiency. Their own good judgment may always be relied upon. They are careful, meticulous, alert.

In reality, your office or place of business is doubtlessly a little less Utopia-like. From time to time, mistakes *do* occur. Subordinates *are* sometimes careless. They do *not* always do the things you would like them to do in the way you would prefer. They must occasionally backtrack, check on instructions, redo their work.

In short, they are human beings—and, thus, imperfect.

That being so, you would be less than human yourself if you did not criticize them when they err.

But does your criticism work . . . or simply cause resentment? If you suspect that your criticism of others is not as effective as it might be, possibly you could profit from a brief reminder about:

THE PURPOSE OF CRITICISM

Why should you criticize a man? Because you are displeased with him? Because your own ego requires boosting? Because you need an outlet for your hostilities?

No.

The only proper reasons for criticizing another are:

1. To prevent the recurrence of a particular pattern of behavior.
2. To increase on-the-job performance.

Before we turn to the simple rules for giving criticism, however, it might be helpful to see how effective a critic you are now. Does your criticism make people want to improve—or is it more apt to make them want to "get even" with you? Here is a little quiz that will divulge any weak spots in the way you now point out mistakes to others.

	YES	NO
1. When a snafu occurs, do you tend to assume who is at fault?	☐	☐
2. Do you "talk down" to subordinates who have goofed?	☐	☐
3. Do you do your best to uncover *all* the facts behind an error?	☐	☐
4. Are you always in control of your temper when criticizing others?	☐	☐
5. Do you habitually talk things over with the "culprit" in private?	☐	☐
6. Do you ever share the responsibility for another's error?	☐	☐
7. When criticizing another, do you make an honest effort to suggest concrete steps he can take to avoid repeating his mistakes?	☐	☐

	YES	NO
8. Do you believe that there are times when only an old-fashioned "chewing out" gets results?	☐	☐
9. Do you commend before you criticize?	☐	☐
10. Do you studiously avoid mentioning names when you criticize?	☐	☐

If you are the perfect critic, you should have checked YES opposite questions 3, 4, 5, 6, 7, 9 and 10 and NO opposite questions 1, 2 and 8. If you are not perfect, you can improve by observing these simple rules:

GET ALL THE PERTINENT FACTS

One of the costliest boners made by executives in their dealings with the people under them is to confuse facts with personalities. Instead of investigating the cold truth behind employee mistakes, they blame one or another of the offender's personality traits.

But consider the fact that one of the chief functions of criticism is *to prevent the recurrence of a particular pattern of behavior*. Isn't it, therefore, logical to acquaint yourself thoroughly with that pattern of behavior *before* you leap to conclusions?

Suppose, for example, that your secretary cannot find an important document that she filed away last month. Your goal is to prevent her from misfiling any more documents. How would you accomplish that?

First, you would recall if she had ever misfiled any other documents. You might ask her to describe her method of filing, then request a demonstration. You would check to see whether anyone else had access to her files. You might even ask whether anybody else had occasion to take the document out of the file. Additional avenues of investigation might suggest themselves to you. Only after you had collected all possible pertinent information would you be in a position to assess the situation and intelligently criticize your secretary. Then—and only then—could you help her avoid misfiling documents in the future.

Since many of the facts that you need can only be supplied by the person you will be criticizing, you must learn to get them from him (or her) with a minimum of friction.

The cardinal rule here is: *leave out all personal remarks.* Avoid using anyone's name. Instead, simply ask, "What happened?" This approach immediately eliminates the person involved and zeroes in on the mistake itself.

Some examples: "We've never had any trouble with that machine before—what happened?" "I can't remember the last time a customer complained about a misrouted order—what happened?" "This is the first accident of its kind here—what happened?"

With personalities thus eliminated from the conversation, you stand a far better chance of getting the bare facts behind the mistake. And facts alone will tell you what the real problem is.

REMAIN CALM

Admittedly, it isn't always easy to control your temper, but aside from the immediate relief "blowing your stack" may give you, what does it accomplish?

Very little. More often than not, it only creates tension on both sides; tension, in turn, triggers hostility; and hostility usually manifests itself in aggression. Net result: everyone involved grows bitter, vindictive, spiteful. Nothing positive or constructive is accomplished.

But consider the effects of allowing yourself some time in which to cool off before approaching the offender. You're calm. So is he. You can face each other coolly and rationally discuss exactly "what happened." By keeping your words moderate and aimed at the facts, you create a climate of sweet reasonableness in which the other fellow will be encouraged to work with you against the common foe: an error.

CRITICIZE IN PRIVATE

Some time ago, in order to measure the precise effects of varying forms of criticism on human performance, a team of psychologists asked for volunteers at a large university. When they had a sufficient number of subjects, the researchers divided them into seven groups and gave each group the same series of challenging tasks to perform.

As each group completed its first set of tasks, it was briefed on its performance. But each group was told in a different way. One group was praised in front of the others; another was ridiculed in private; still another was publicly reprimanded . . . and so on. The tests were then continued.

In simple chart form, here is a rundown of the performances on that second series of tasks.

Incentive Method Used After First Series of Tests	Percentage Showing Better Results on Second Series of Tests
Public praise	87.5
Private reprimand	66.3
Public reprimand	34.7
Private ridicule	32.5
Public ridicule	17.0
Private sarcasm	27.9
Public sarcasm	11.9

While public praise was the most effective incentive of all, invariably—you will notice—private criticism produced better results than public criticism. That is, the private reprimand outproduced the public reprimand; private ridicule achieved results superior to public ridicule; even sarcasm was far more effective when delivered in private than in public.

The moral for the man who must criticize another would appear to be crystal clear: *keep it private.*

COMMEND BEFORE YOU CRITICIZE

No employee likes to be told that he has committed an error. It is a blow to his pride and a threat to the image of himself as a competent worker that he carries about with him.

Nevertheless, criticism is sometimes called for. *Problem:*

how can you "straighten out" the offender without crippling his own high opinion of himself?

Answer: sugar-coat your criticism by preceding it with a compliment. Be absolutely sure, however, that your prefatory commendation is merited, for employees can usually spot the false compliment before you have even completed it. It is, for example, far better to say, "You handled the Perkins complaint as well as any man in the firm could have, under the circumstances" than to launch into suspicious-sounding superlatives like, "The masterful way in which you handled the Perkins complaint is the greatest example of creative salesmanship I've ever seen!"

By prefacing your criticism with an honest bouquet, you do two things: you assure the employee that you still think highly of him and you indicate that you view his "goof" as an untypical departure from his usual good work. Thus reassured, he is apt to be receptive to what you say.

KEEP IT CONSTRUCTIVE

Since the only valid purposes of criticism are positive in nature, it is only common sense that you keep your criticism positive, too. This is not to deny that it sometimes requires an almost superhuman effort to avoid sarcasm or invective. Some mistakes *are* stupid. Some *do* cost you money, time, energy, customer good-will.

But once an error has been committed, all the shouting in the world will not recoup one iota of your loss. The only sensible thing you can do is to make sure the offender does not repeat his mistake. And the way to accomplish this is by pinpointing, *with his help,* what went wrong and showing him what steps to take to ensure never repeating the error.

Once you make clear to him that the sole purpose of your criticism is to help him become a better worker, he will respond in kind: he will make an honest effort to improve.

And that, really, is what criticism is all about.

Chapter Six

How to Size Up People

It is always an advantage to know as much as possible about the other fellow, whether he is an applicant for a job, a subordinate, a competitor or someone with whom you are doing business—or hope to. For, once you know a man's basic character, his weaknesses and strong points, his interests and goals, you can "tailor" your approach to him accordingly and, usually, place him in the job for which he is best suited—win his cooperation and loyalty—anticipate his reactions to various situations—make him your ally.

Andrew Carnegie was in the habit of throwing tricky theoretical problems in steel manufacturing at men who wished to join his firm. Walter Chrysler frequently gave his executives unexpected vacations, just to see how capably their assistants could assume their responsibilities. J. C. Penney painted unattractive pictures of small-town life to aspiring managers of his store chain in order to see if they really had what it takes.

While you may not wish to go to the lengths that these men did to size up others, there are some readily available clues that can help you understand what makes a man tick. Here are 20 especially revealing ones.

1. WHAT HE OWNS

His car, his home, his clothing—each tells a great deal about his character. The fancy automobile with every possible accessory obviously belongs to a man who sets high store in a "good front." The stripped-down, inexpensive car more likely bespeaks a practical nature. You can learn a lot about a man by paying attention to what he chooses to spend his money on— from cuff links to college educations for his children.

2. WHAT HE LIKES TO DO

A man who frequents museums and libraries may be a "status seeker," but more likely he has a cultural interest in them. A man who vacations at Las Vegas may be there for the climate; more likely, he enjoys gambling and taking chances.

The man who enjoys improving his home, manicuring his lawn and puttering with his car is obviously a different kind of person from the one who prefers to go hunting or mountain climbing and camping on his time off. The first is probably family-oriented, with a strong sense of responsibility—a man who relishes his role as a breadwinner. The second, who may also enjoy his family, is more responsive to challenges, with a leaning toward solitude and self-reliance—something of a loner. It is important to understand that no individual can be compartmentalized as a pure family man or an absolute loner, for everyone is a subtle mixture of many tendencies. But in just about everyone, there is a dominant passion that can, with patience, be pinpointed.

Clearly, two such men are motivated by different considerations. The family man is likely to respond to an approach that appeals to his dependability. The loner would be more apt to react positively to a "this-is-the-situation-we-leave-it-to-you" gambit.

Regardless of the identity of the man whom you are trying to size up, remember: hobbies and leisure-time activities are solid clues to his make-up.

3. HOW HE SPEAKS

Careful speech, with good grammar and correct pronunciation, implies thoughtfulness, education, an appreciation of logic. Careless speech, on the other hand, suggests equally careless habits of thinking.

4. WHAT HE READS

Is he interested in expanding his own horizons, learning more about his own specialty, furthering his career? He's ambitious. Is he pretty much a newspaper-and-general-magazine reader? He probably cares less about getting ahead. Of course, the demands of time are often a factor here, but those who want to read somehow manage to find the time.

5. WHAT HE LIKES TO TALK ABOUT

There is at least one group of specialists whose primary job is listening to others. They talk only when absolutely necessary and even then it is usually to pose a question so that the speaker may continue his near-soliloquy.

These specialists, of course, are psychoanalysts. By not setting any limits on *what* their patients may talk about, they discover what is uppermost in their minds, for when people are left to their own devices, sooner or later they speak of the things that count to them.

Take a tip from the psychoanalyst—from time to time, let your people choose the subject of conversation. There will be a great deal of irrelevant small talk, to be sure, but eventually a topic of true and abiding interest to the speaker will emerge. When it does, take mental notes. They will be invaluable clues to what makes him really tick.

Obviously, you don't have all the time in the world in which to enter into a psychoanalytical session with an employee, but whenever the opportunity does present itself, seize it and encourage your people to open up to you. It can be highly revealing.

6. WHOM HE ADMIRES

Sooner or later, men talk about the people whose characters, personalities and achievements they look up to. Some find those who took the ruthless road to power admirable; others prefer the world's humanitarians. One man may admire a particular businessman; another, a leading athlete. Jones may find vicarious satisfaction in the exploits of whatever playboy is currently in the headlines. Smith may feel that the astronauts personify all the worthwhile virtues. Get a man to tell you whom he admires and you have gone a long way toward sizing him up.

7. WHAT HIS DOMINANT INTEREST IS

Politics? Economics? Horse racing? The Civil War? Making money? Whatever it is, it is a signpost of his character.

8. HOW HE TREATS OTHERS

If he is in a position of authority, does he conduct himself like a little Caesar or does he respect the rights of others? If he works under another, does he manage to cooperate without stooping to apple polishing? Does he give credit where credit is due or is he a "glory hog"? Is he a buck-passer, a rumor monger, or a character assassin? Real character can frequently be assessed by noting how a man treats the people with whom he comes into contact daily.

9. WHICH ACCOMPLISHMENTS HE'S PROUDEST OF

Find out what a man considers his most important achievements and you have a master key to his character. If he recalls with relish, for example, how he solved a particularly knotty problem, you may safely assume that he would tackle other challenges with enthusiasm and ability. If he cites a penchant for leading others, he would probably react well to appeals to his sense of responsibility. If he takes pride in the accomplishments of his department or firm, he is probably a strong believer in team effort and cooperation.

10. WHAT HIS SELF-IMAGE IS

One of the few men able to influence President Wilson was Colonel Edward House. Why? Because early in their relationship, House discovered that Wilson could not stand being told what to do by anyone. Somewhat childishly, the President was incapable of admitting that his knowledge of any subject was insufficient or limited.

"After I got to know Mr. Wilson," House once reported, "I learned that the best way to convert him to an idea was to plant it in his mind casually, but so as to interest him in it, so as to get him thinking about it on his own account. The first time this worked it was an accident. I had been visiting with him at the White House and urged a policy on him which he appeared to disapprove. But several days later, at the dinner table, I was amazed to hear him trot out my suggestion as his own."

It was largely in this way that House established his tremendous hold over Woodrow Wilson.

Why?

Because Colonel House was keen enough to recognize President Wilson's "self-image," that of a totally self-sufficient, completely knowledgeable man, and then use it when he thought it necessary.

To some extent, each of us entertains a somewhat distorted notion of the kind of person he is. And this "self-image" is a reliable clue to our characters. Learn what a man's "self-image" is, how he sees himself, and you have one important key to what makes him tick.

One man, for example, may picture himself as the epitome of all the major virtues, a born leader, better than most people. Another may view himself as possessed of a keen analytical mind, unswayed by emotional considerations. A third may entertain an image of himself as a great innovator and idea man.

As a general rule, people tend to respond positively to those external forces that affirm their own opinions of themselves and negatively to those external forces that deny their "self-images."

If you wanted three such men to wear their safety helmets

on the job, for example, you would be wise to approach them in terms of their individual "self-images."

To the first, your most effective appeal might be, "Everybody looks up to you, Joe. If you made a point of wearing the helmet, the others would follow your lead."

To the second, the approach that worked best might go, "These helmets have reduced head injuries more than 90 percent wherever they've been used in our industry, Harry. Don't you agree that they're worth using?"

The third man would be most apt to respond to something like this: "You're a bright guy, George. I don't have to draw pictures for you on the subject of safety. These helmets have tested out and we want all you men to take advantage of the latest safety equipment."

What have you really done in each case? You've put what you want done in terms of each man's "self-image."

A bit childish? Maybe. Immature? Perhaps.

But it works like a charm.

11. WHAT HIS GOALS IN LIFE ARE

Find out what a man has his eye on, to what objectives he is bending his energies and you can usually deduce the dominant strain in his character. Is he aiming for a certain income? A better job? Early retirement? Fame in his chosen field? Power? Or does he consider other pursuits—helping others, working for a better community—more important? Whatever his goals, you can probably influence him by putting your instructions or propositions in terms of this major interest.

12. WHAT HIS WORK AREA IS LIKE

Whether it's a humble workshop cubicle or an impressive, gadget-equipped office, a man's work area is a solid clue to his make-up. Neat? He probably is orderly in other ways. Well furnished? He likes people to recognize that he has "arrived." Plaques, degrees, assorted mementoes on the wall frequently indicate his major interests and of which achievements he is proudest.

13. WHAT IDEAS HE CONTRIBUTES

An employee who habitually suggests ways to save time or money is involved with his work and probably more ambitious than the employee who single-mindedly does his job. Even if his ideas are not always good ones, or entirely practical, their existence signifies a thinking man. Of course, if the ideas are continually absurd or overly complicated, the man may simply enjoy hearing himself talk. Imagination is rare enough to warrant encouragement wherever it is found, but it must be at least tinged with basic reasonableness. The "idea man" is apt to be enthusiastic by nature, impatient with having things spelled out for him. His cooperation is best won by explaining clearly what is expected of him, then leaving him to his own devices as much as possible.

14. WHAT MAKES HIM LAUGH

Humor is one important safety valve for the venting of human emotion. The man who never opens this valve may be allowing too much hostility to build up in himself. When it does finally manifest itself, it may take the form of overt anti-social behavior like hatred or violence. In particular, look out for the man without a capacity for laughing at himself—he is in deep psychological trouble, rigid in his thinking and lacking in the ability to see his own shortcomings. Conversely, the man who makes himself the butt of all his jokes may really have a very low opinion of himself. Two such different types, naturally, have to be handled quite differently.

15. HOW HE REACTS TO CHALLENGES

There is a certain breed of man that thrives on the untested and untried. Such men find within themselves untapped resources upon which they can draw to meet new responsibilities head on. Is there a problem? They'll dig for the solution until they find it. Is there a better way to do something? They'll experiment until they hit upon it. "Can't" is not in their vocabulary.

There is another sort. These men never dream of sticking out their necks, of striking out from shore. The *status quo* is their haven and once they have been shown the standard procedure for accomplishing something, that is their way for all time. The new approach, the daring departure, the added responsibility are not for them. Challenge? That's for oddballs. Can't? It's their basic philosophy.

The challenge-meeters are almost always tougher to manage than the duckers, but put what you want done in terms geared to capture their imaginations and you will have to look long and hard for more highly motivated employees.

16. HOW HE REACTS TO SETBACKS

How a man takes a rebuff speaks volumes about him. If he is intelligent and well balanced, he won't sulk (for long), but will try to learn from his failure. He doesn't seek to blame others for it, but prefers to look forward rather than harp on the unhappy past. If he dwells on it, boring those around him with endless excuses and quick to take offense at any mention of his setback, he is not as mature as he should be. Such men are not ready for large responsibilities.

17. HOW HE REACHES A DECISION

The way in which a man makes up his mind to pursue a certain course of action is another clue to his psychic make-up. A thoughtful, prudent person will gather as much data as possible, consult with others, study all the "angles" before acting. An impulsive person will act hastily, often overlooking several possibilities.

18. WHAT HIS GRIPES ARE

What irritates a man can be a key to his character. If he objects to reasonable regulations, for example, he may lack self-confidence. If, on the other hand, his complaints are usually justified and not too frequently lodged, he is probably a well-adjusted individual. The man who thinks others are being favored over himself—whose gripes center on the authority others have over him—who sees "conspiracies" on every side may have a personality problem such as delusions of persecution. Such an individual may require professional help.

Gripes, of course, can be healthy outlets for high spirits and many are expressed simply as a form of friendly bantering, actually signifying good morale. They can be discounted.

What genuinely disturbs a man, however, should be considered in your total assessment of his character.

19. HOW HE ACCEPTS PRAISE AND CRITICISM

A compliment may spur one worker to new heights of achievement, but only inflate the ego of another. Some men can take praise and put it to work for them, using it as a secret source of energy and inspiration for additional accomplishment. Others view it as a signal to coast on their reputations. Watch how an employee takes a pat on the back—it tells a great deal about his level of maturity.

The other side of the coin—criticism—can be even more revealing. Nobody likes to hear that he has made a mistake, but the serious worker will accept criticism as a springboard to improved performance by taking whatever steps are necessary to assure that he won't repeat his error. The less stable man, who may lack self-confidence, will bridle at the mere suggestion that he goofed. He may try to place the blame elsewhere. In extreme cases, he may even accuse his critic of hidden motives. Such a man is not ready for advancement.

20. WHAT HIS PERSONAL MANNERISMS ARE

Most of us have little habits that provide insights into what makes us tick. The chain smoker usually works under pressure. The "conversation hog" tends to be self-centered. The table drummer often lacks patience. In particular, watch what a man does with his hands. They are unconscious clues to character.

These 20 keys to "reading" a human being are not infallible, of course, but they are among the major signals that your people send out to you, from which you may deduce their character. To the extent that you read those signals shrewdly and tailor your own approach to the individuals whom you manage, to that extent you will improve your own performance and, consequently, theirs.

Chapter Seven

Get the Most Out of Your Employees' Idea Power

Just as the average individual works at no more than 15–20 percent of his true potential, so do most companies operate on a mere fraction of the idea power at their disposal.

What these firms overlook is the vast pool of know-how and creative thought under their noses: their employees.

Yet, ideas have always been important to business. Today they are crucial. With competition—and costs—growing tougher on all fronts, in order to survive, compete and thrive, no company can have too many ideas from which to draw. The man at the lathe, the girl at the typewriter, the firing line salesman— each, in his way, is an expert whose experience and ideas represent a deep reservoir of know-how. Why not tap this well of knowledge for the benefit of all?

True—some firms do, in the form of a suggestion box or periodical contests. But precious few companies have any real program for the continuous, purposeful mining of the latent creativity of their employees.

The responsibility—and failure—is management's. Busy with a hundred other problems, the men on top tend to assign a low priority (if any) to unearthing good ideas from their rank and file. They will hold a meeting of department heads at the drop of a hat, think nothing of hiring $500-a-day consultants (who may know very little and understand less about their specific needs), or stylishly pin their hopes on a million-dollar computer to solve their problems.

But ask an employee, who knows intimately the problems of his day-to-day job, for help? Pshaw!

As a manager, you can alter this situation in your own company or department by understanding the nature of creativity, recognizing the untapped potential all around you and establishing the kind of atmosphere in which the "creative thrust" of your subordinates is encouraged.

Here, specifically, is what you can do.

ENCOURAGE INDIVIDUAL THINKING

Everything, from the type in which you are reading this to the product your company manufactures or distributes, was once only an idea in somebody's head. A couple of bicycle mechanics fathered the aviation industry. A dreamy-eyed putterer invented the telephone. A former candy-butcher was responsible for the movie, phonograph, and lighting industries.

Were the Wright Brothers, Alexander Graham Bell, or Thomas Edison starting out today as employees of some large organization, it is highly problematical whether their fantastic dreams would ever reach the front office. Fortunately, they were highly individualistic men who believed in their ideas. Refusing to be discouraged by all the "proofs" that their schemes could never work, they stubbornly stuck to their guns. Result: each revolutionized the world in which he lived.

Very few people are gifted with the single-minded devotion to an idea that these giants possessed. And though you may not have a potential Edison on your work force, there is almost surely at least one man (or woman) who, right now, is asking himself, "Suppose we did things this way instead of that way?"

And for every worker who is consciously playing with a new idea, there are two or more who would be glad to try if they knew you cared.

So let them know you *do* care. Tell them that you realize

they know more about their specific jobs than anybody else—including you. Explain that you recognize there is always room for improvement and you are relying on them to pinpoint such things as the wasting of money and time, better ways to accomplish their tasks, more productive methods to replace current routines.

Whenever possible, ask specific questions:

"How can we cut the time between order and delivery?"

"What's the real cause of that quality problem?"

"How can we increase sales by 20 percent next year?"

By giving your employees concrete problems to tackle, you will give them something to zero in on with their brains.

To be sure, you will get a lot of worthless, even bad, ideas. But you will get a few that are not so bad. And, every once in a while, you will be handed a gem on a silver platter.

Most importantly, you will be inculcating your workers with the habit of "looking for trouble."

That's where the best ideas come from.

DON'T BE AN IDEA STIFLER

Unwittingly, a lot of executives are idea killers. Some are snobs who think, "If Jones could dream up good ideas, he wouldn't be a shipping clerk in the first place." But everybody has to start someplace. Jones just might have the answer to cutting your traffic costs. He deserves a hearing.

Others are so mundane in their own thinking that they are jealous of anyone who shows a spark of creativity.

Still others don't want to rock the boat—view every idea as a threat to their own position—honestly, but erroneously, believe that theirs is the best of all possible worlds.

And there are those who have difficulty in recognizing a good idea when they see one. Unless the idea is presented in highly polished, flawless form, they dismiss it as worthless.

The solution? Take stock of yourself as a judge of ideas. If, upon analysis, you discover that you tend to quash ideas for any reason besides their lack of intrinsic merit, consciously try to suppress the personal prejudices that are costing you good ideas.

SUSPEND YOUR CRITICAL JUDGMENT

A creative thought is sometimes hampered in its early stages because the form in which it initially appears may be weak and ineffectual. The originator of the idea may have a poor command of language, be unable to express his thoughts persuasively—even have a squeaky voice.

But don't confuse the presentation with the idea itself. A chemist with only a so-so ability for self-expression may pop up with the ideal solution to a problem in distillation. The painfully shy accountant who stutters *could* come up with a new way to finance your expansion program. The young girl in the typing pool, despite her inability to make it crystal clear, may know a way to get correspondence out faster.

Even "wild notions" may contain the germ of solid thinking—if you can separate the wheat from the chaff.

That's why it is important that you view *every* idea as a potential winner. Granted, to turn an idea into usable shape, you may have to add, subtract, modify or combine it with additional ideas. In such a case your original idea may, in retrospect, become merely a jumping-off point. But without it, you would get nowhere.

Be slow, therefore, to condemn any idea to oblivion. If it is not feasible today, it may be eminently practical tomorrow or next year. Even if it appears unusable, the "secret ingredient" needed to transform it into solid gold may pop up in the future.

KEEP THE CHANNELS OF COMMUNICATION OPEN

If there is any one reason why employees are reluctant to submit ideas "up the line," it is *red tape*. Too often, in order to get an idea to the proper man, a worker has to put it in writing (possibly in triplicate), make a hard-to-get appointment, pursue his supervisor or boss as if he were seeking a favor instead of conferring one.

There are several ways in which you can make it easy for your employees' ideas to come to you.

You can establish certain hours during which an "open-door" policy prevails in your office—any employee can drop in unannounced to talk an idea over with you.

You can design a simple printed form on which ideas can be submitted to you in writing. Suggestion: keep it down to one page. Long forms discourage people.

You can make individual appointments with people to discuss their brainstorms. An appointment makes people feel important—proves you are anxious to hear them out—suggests that you consider their ideas as vital as any of your other business. Be sure, however, that such appointments are not difficult to get, and that you honor them, regardless of other pressures. An idea-man snubbed can be very sensitive. Possibly to the point of keeping his good ideas to himself.

FOLLOW THROUGH ON IDEAS

A man's idea is like a woman's child. He wants to know how his "baby" is doing at all times.

Don't disappoint him. Attend promptly to the ideas that your people come up with and provide them with regular feedback on what is happening to their ideas, when they are going to be evaluated and by whom.

If the idea is under serious consideration, tell the originator so. If it has run into some problem, explain that, too. If certain flaws have cropped up, describe them; he may have the answer. At the very least, he will understand why his idea is not being adopted.

The important thing is to prove to your employees that all their ideas are taken seriously. Thus assured, they will do their best to come up with more—and better—ideas.

GIVE RECOGNITION

You like to get credit for your ideas. So do your employees. Be quick, therefore, to show appreciation for good work and see to it that individuals receive the proper acknowledgment for their ideas, whether it takes the form of a bonus, prize, raise, scroll—or the simple public expression, "Well done!"

Such rewards are not only just and proper; they are extremely practical. Recognition tends to raise employee standards. Next time they will try to equal or surpass the good job they did this time. And those who witness the recognition will be spurred on to greater effort. A little friendly competition never hurt anyone.

The encouragement of ideas among your subordinates pays a double dividend. It improves the competitive posture of your company by reducing costs, increasing profits and permitting every employee to perform more closely to his true potential. And it makes every job—including yours—more challenging, more exciting, more fun.

BE A POSITIVE LISTENER

To be an effective generator of ideas in others, you must possess a bouncy optimism yourself, the attitude that Dr. Johnson epitomized when he said, "There is not a problem the human mind can conceive that the human mind cannot also solve." Such an attitude is contagious. It infects those around you with the determination to come up with good ideas.

A positive listener hears out an idea—any idea—in order to see whether there is even an iota of possibility in it. If there is, he points it out to the originator and suggests further lines of pursuit and development.

For example, an employee suggests, "Why don't we buy and renovate the old building next door and use it to lick our space shortage?" You know that it isn't a practical idea now because of a budget cut. But instead of simply turning thumbs down and discouraging the employee from any further attempts to be of help, you say, "Not a bad idea, but we can't swing it now, I'm afraid. Why don't you see whether there is any portion of this building that can be fixed up for storage?" Meanwhile, you file the original idea for possible implementation when money is less tight. *Result:* the originator of the idea is encouraged to continue looking for solutions and is pleased with himself for obviously having made a contribution.

If the idea is downright bad, explain *why* as tactfully as you can—and encourage the employee to keep trying. Point out the factors he has overlookd in his thinking: consequences that may not have occurred to him or recent developments he may not be aware of. His very next idea may be just what you have been looking for.

Chapter Eight

How to Generate Excitement Among Your Employees

It isn't difficult to spot the employee who considers his firm a winner. He arrives at work on time, if not earlier; knows what is expected of him—and tries to do more; pitches in on jobs not even always in his area of responsibility; and, at the end of the day, has plenty to talk about to his wife. He may even boast about his company to friends and neighbors. He respects his fellow workers, has confidence in his management, feels that he is really part of a team.

There is another kind of employee. He comes to work on time, but not a minute earlier; does his job, but not a scintilla more; leaves precisely at 5 P.M. and as the door shuts behind him, so does his work. If his wife asks him what he did that day, he is apt to grunt some monosyllabic acknowledgment or ignore the question altogether. He considers his fellows just as trapped from 9 to 5 as he is, tends to envy management its "soft jobs" and considers the company a necessary evil at best, a powerful opponent at worst.

Obviously, it is the first type of employee who makes companies prosper. It is his loyalty, his best efforts, his enthusiasm for his job and his firm that is literally the backbone of his company's success.

The management that succeeds in convincing its workers that they are part of a winning combination is the management that usually finds that its employees are comprised primarily of the first type.

How, precisely, can you build this winning, "going somewhere" spirit into your employees?

There is no single, magic formula. Rather, a combination of techniques is required, based partly on effective communications, partly on a sincere interest in your workers, partly on your personal enthusiasm for the future.

Here are some steps you can take right now to cultivate a current of vitality in your own organization.

FIND OUT WHAT'S EXCITING

Obviously, before you can generate excitement in your people, you must have something solid with which to excite them.

Consider, for a moment, the kind of news that might impress you: the beating out of a competitor; the cracking of a new market for your product; the landing of a big customer or contract; a research breakthrough; the development of a new procedure, patent or product; some form of recognition by the outside world.

Well, if these things interest you, why wouldn't they interest the people who work for you?

To the production line worker responsible for only one small operation, it means a great deal to learn that the product he works on is considered superior to competitive products. If he learns that "his" product has been chosen over another or is now being used by another company as a component in a bigger product, it is not only a tribute to his personal competence; it proves that he was smart to join your company in the first place. His good judgment is being confirmed.

The salesman who hears of the advances being made by your researchers feels that his efforts are being backed up by technological innovation. This knowledge keeps him enthusiastic and translates itself into better selling, for an enthusiastic salesman kindles customers and prospects alike.

So keep your eyes and ears open for any news that isn't restricted information, whether it is a government citation, an editorial in a local newspaper praising your firm, the introduction of a new product or new policy, or whatever.

Almost anything that is happening to or in your firm or any of its departments is of interest to some, if not all, your employees.

Of course, there will be days—even weeks and months—that are strictly routine. Most business operations *are* routine. Companies could not otherwise function.

But still there are ways to generate excitement. Who, for example, has surpassed his past performance? Which departments have been meeting—and beating—their quotas? Who has earned special recognition, special bonuses, special privileges?

The good things you bring to the attention of your employees need not always concern them personally. It is frequently enough to prove to them that something exciting is happening to somebody else. So long as they feel that there is possibility in the air, that lightning can strike them at any time, that knowledge in itself will often ignite their imaginations and trigger a "winning" psychology.

An employee, for example, suggests a new office procedure. For his trouble, he is awarded a $50 Savings Bond. "If he can do it, so can I," think his fellows—and are happy for him as well as for their own future good ideas.

FIND OUT WHAT'S BOTHERING THEM

An employee who is irritated by what he considers bad treatment, poor communications or unfair policies cannot consider his firm a friend or even an employer worthy of his loyalty.

Since the overwhelming majority of grievances is usually the result of the worker lacking sufficient information, the surest way to avoid this costly sulking is to encourage employees to speak up and tell management what is on their minds, then have management explain fully, where possible, the reasons for the treatment, policies or whatever the bone of contention may be.

Some large companies go to considerable expense to encourage this two-way communications, providing printed forms for employee grievances, assuring anonymity by funneling all complaints through one man only (he forwards the complaint anonymously to management and sees to it that management's reply reaches the proper worker) and directing managers to take the time to answer all complaints fully.

If the complaint is found to be justified, of course, suitable remedial action is taken.

In one such case, an employee was put out because a fellow worker appeared to have been promoted over him unfairly. In view of the firm's established policy of promoting men of equal merit according to seniority, and the apparent fact that he outranked the promoted man, the employee frankly felt cheated. He put his grievance in writing and, within 48 hours, received a full explanation: the promoted man had joined the company after the complainer, true, but prior to his employment there had worked for seven years for a firm that had later merged with the parent company. By the terms of the merger, all employees of the merged firm were to be credited for the years they had worked there. In fact, therefore, the promoted man had four years of seniority over the employee filing the grievance.

Net result of this candid two-way communication: a satisfied employee who now knows that his company "plays fair."

Your own grievance program can be less formal. A simple invitation to employees to let you know what's bothering them, together with assurances that no complaint will be held against them, will often do the trick. If there are no takers, assume the initiative by scheduling individual meetings with your people at three- or six-month intervals and, behind closed doors, ask them confidentially whether there is anything on their minds.

Such a program may initially meet with some skepticism, but eventually your people will appreciate what you are trying to do and they will open up.

APPLY THE GOLDEN RULE

Inculcating subordinates with enthusiasm for their jobs and company can't be achieved by wishful thinking. It takes skill and patience, and giving to your people what you yourself want.

For example, you appreciate praise and recognition. Then why not give it where it is deserved? You like to get credit for your ideas. If one of your subordinates comes up with a good one—even if it's not completely worked out—give him credit for it. You'll be on your way to creating an enthusiastic worker.

You like clean-cut work assignments. If you like to know exactly what you are expected to do, why not delegate work in the same clear manner?

You like to understand the "why" of what you are doing. Then wouldn't it boost a subordinate's interest and desire to cooperate if you explained the purpose of his part of the job and where it fits into the total picture?

You like an attentive and understanding listener. When one of your people has something to say to you, he would doubtlessly appreciate your really listening to him, too.

You like the management policies that direct your activities to be consistent and well thought out, for nothing is so demoralizing as poorly planned policies that head in one direction today and shift tomorrow. Look at your policies toward your subordinates in this light.

Finally, you like to work for someone you respect. It brings out the best in most people. Everyone likes to feel that his boss knows his job and is giving his best to it every day. Do your own job as well as you possibly can, therefore, not only because you ought to, but because of the example it sets for those who look to you for guidance.

USE THE BARNUM TOUCH

The creation of employee excitement depends essentially on managerial deeds, to be sure, but unless those deeds are brought to the attention of employees, they will have been substantially in vain.

In other words, you must not only do the right things; you must do them with some fanfare, some drama, a touch of P. T. Barnum.

This is not to say that you must exaggerate or ring bells prior to every announcement. It does mean that you should make sure that the exciting things in your firm are publicized through every means at your disposal. Some suggestions:

BULLETIN BOARDS—these are natural outlets for such news as promotions, additions to the work force, routine messages from the president and vacation schedules.

MEMOS—from time to time, some special event takes place —a company-sponsored social gathering, for example—that ought to be brought to the attention of everyone. Since bulletin boards are not always consulted by all employees, the memo is a surer way of getting the news to each person.

HOUSE ORGAN—the house organ should not be merely a catalog of births, retirements and bowling scores. It should keep everyone informed about what the company is doing and create a sense of vitality. This is the place to reprint magazine or newspaper articles about your firm. If journalists are interested in what your company is doing, let your employees know about it. If nothing else, it boosts pride in the company. Speeches by company officers, reprinted in your house organ, can stimulate interest—particularly if they are discussions of the firm's achievements or blueprints for future achievements.

LETTERS—those written by top management to cite individual workers' achievements are of particular value because they indicate that the "front office" knows what's going on throughout the firm—and cares. Some firms go even further: as a matter of policy, not only is every special individual contribution recognized by a letter addressed to the employee's desk or workbench, but his wife receives a letter at home explaining how proud the firm is to have her husband on its team. Needless to say, every wife is thrilled to hear that her husband is considered an important man. And no man is unhappy to emerge a hero in his wife's eyes.

Basically, the creation of the kind of electric excitement that makes companies successful depends on the extent to which management is itself excited and how well it communicates its excitement to its people.

With that in mind, it might not be a bad idea to take stock of your own attitudes and methods right now.

Chapter Nine

Winning Cooperation from Employees

More than 40 years ago, Henry Ford said, "The ability to lead others is the single most important trait a businessman can possess."

To this day, top executives agree. In a survey conducted by a well-known management association, a cross-section of American managers were asked to pinpoint the one personal characteristic they considered most essential to a man who wanted to succeed in business. The overwhelming consensus: "The ability to work with—and through—people."

Employees themselves back this up daily by willingly doing their best for some bosses while begrudgingly turning out a day's work for others.

What makes the difference?

In a nutshell, the bosses themselves. The smart ones have mastered the art of winning their employees' cooperation.

Have you? If you have, you can tell easily enough. Your employees are prompt, cheerful, ready to put in that extra lick.

If you haven't, you can tell that easily enough, too. Your employees are tardy, unmotivated, dash madly for the door at 5 P.M.

More often than not, your people's attitude and performance mirror your own. For, as in most things in life, "you get what you give."

Certainly, no manager is perfect. He has his own problems, neuroses, and biases to contend with. He has disagreements with his wife, misunderstandings with his children, mortgage payments to meet, traffic jams to stew over, the day's headlines to contemplate and a hundred petty annoyances nipping at his heels daily. It would be unrealistic to expect him not to be affected by them and, occasionally, to "give" less than he should.

Yet, it may be helpful to contemplate a standard of excellence, if only to have some way of measuring your own performance. If we could somehow poll all the employees in the world—and top management, too—for their ideas of the ideal manager, Mr. Perfection would probably come out something like this.

HE GIVES EFFECTIVE WORK ASSIGNMENTS

He knows which of his people respond best to brief, one-at-a-time tasks and which work best under broader gauge assignments. He doesn't set artificially high time pressures, although he understands the value of setting reasonable target dates for assignments that might otherwise stretch out. He anticipates the need for new assignments, stockpiling work assignments so he will be ready when his people complete current ones. At the same time, he schedules work breathers, setting aside time for jobs that need doing such as cleaning out files, maintaining records or reviewing procedures.

HE HELPS HIS PEOPLE GROW

Because loyalty is a two-way street, he fights for his people when necessary. If a raise is merited, for example, he sees to it that the deserving employee receives it. He informs his people of openings within the company to which they may aspire. He never tries to hold back a good man, even if it means transfer into another department. In a hundred little ways, he lets his people know that he will go to bat for them.

HE PLAYS UP THE POSITIVE

He recognizes that just as praise is a better stimulant than criticism, so appreciation is better than a lack of it and building up a person's self-respect gets more results than tearing it down. In building up the self-esteem of his juniors, he builds capable assistants. And, in the long run, this makes his own work easier.

HE NEVER BELITTLES A SUBORDINATE

He understands the damage it can do. There are times when throttling an employee appears to be the only valid option a manager has. In view of the risks involved, however, most managers choose the verbal equivalent of murder, which is disparagement of a man's abilities. It's bad strategy, for you can accuse a man of almost anything—negligence, laziness, forgetfulness—and not damage his ego. But call him "Stupid," even indirectly, and you shatter that which he prizes most highly: his image of himself as a competent, even superior, worker.

HE NEVER PLAYS FAVORITES

He knows that as soon as you start making exceptions because of personal preference, especially when the person you favor is playing up to you, the rest of the staff adopts a what's-the-use attitude. Morale—and motivation—go into a tailspin.

HE GIVES HIS PEOPLE HIS UNDIVIDED ATTENTION

He does not hound them or continually breathe down their necks, but periodically makes it his business to spend some time with every person who reports to him. When a question, problem or complaint is brought to his attention, he invites the man involved into his office and, in privacy, gives him his complete attention for however long may be warranted by the circumstances. He doesn't let the telephone, his secretary or anyone else disturb him.

HE AVOIDS DOMINATION

It only breeds yes-men. An over-forceful boss and subordinates with initiative simply don't get along. If the chief insists on running everything, the best of his people will get out and the rest will let him do their work. The able executive thinks of his staff as working *with* him, not *for* him.

HE COMMUNICATES

Since the aim of effective communications is to reach the *mind* of another person, he selects words suited to that person's level of intelligence, background and experience. If the nature of his communication requires the use of jargon, he makes sure his audience understands the specialized meaning attached to the words he is using. He defines his terms, is brief without being cryptic, avoids abstractions whenever possible.

WHEN HE GOOFS, HE ADMITS IT

He doesn't rationalize away errors, look for scapegoats or sulk. No worker expects his boss to be infallible, so no executive loses face when he admits he's wrong—so long as he isn't wrong too often! What he gains is confidence in his fairness and honesty, an asset beyond price to any executive.

HE FOLLOWS UP AND FOLLOWS THROUGH

Too often, after a program has been developed and launched, a decision made and resources committed, nothing more happens. Many managers feel that their role in a project ends right then and there. This is not the case with the ideal executive. In translating the idea for a new program into effective action, he not only proves the program's worth; he proves his own.

HE ANTICIPATES CHANGE

He understands and welcomes change, for no company, and no job within a company, that remains the same can be thought of as a success. The very moment he feels he has mastered every nuance of his position, he knows, is the moment to question whether he hasn't outgrown it. With this attitude, he can instill the feeling in people that change is to be welcomed, even sought out.

HE PINPOINTS PRIORITIES

He understands that in order to be effective he must continually establish hierarchies of importance: what must be done today, what decisions should be made first, what can wait, what requires additional information, who ought to be consulted, what should be communicated down, or communicated up. In short, he concentrates on the important things—in the order of their importance.

WHEN IN DOUBT, HE QUESTIONS

He doesn't consider company policies and practices inviolable. Rather, he believes that a company's posture and philosophy should constantly be tested in the marketplace and in daily interaction among employees. When a situation is obviously out of line, he knows, "policy" should never be an excuse for inaction. The "book," after all, is full of rules that once supplanted others and may, in turn, be due for revision at any time. None of the rules, the ideal executive realizes, is so sacred that it cannot be questioned.

HE LOOKS BEYOND HIS COMPANY

By joining outside organizations, he broadens his interests and his knowledge. He gets to know himself better throughout the range and depth of his personality—his blind spots as well as his insights. Whether it be in civic or professional activities, the community gets to know him as a responsible, concerned citizen who also works for the ABC Company. The association does the firm no harm. And, by his example, he may well instill similar attitudes on the part of his people.

HE IS DECISIVE

He is willing and able to assume the responsibility for his assessment of the facts in any given situation, once he is satisfied that he has gathered all the pertinent data. Consequently, his subordinates are also confident and motivated to assume responsibility.

HE IS FLEXIBLE

Because business conditions and personal circumstances change so swiftly in this jet-propelled age, he knows how vital it is that he keep his mind and spirit flexible. That means he willingly reexamines firmly held positions in the light of any new information that may be available, he seeks alternative approaches to problems rather than adopting the first one that is suggested or pops into his mind, he tries to fit his approach to people and problems on an individual basis, he refuses to see issues solely in terms of black and white, but has a mind marked by what has been called a "tolerance for ambiguity," an ability to discern gray areas.

HE STRUCTURES SOME SOLITUDE FOR HIMSELF

He knows the importance of a chance to ponder and plan, minus the distractions that ordinarily intrude upon him. Aware that one of the most valuable contributions he can make to his company is creative thought, he appreciates the need for reflective contemplation and planning.

HE CONCENTRATES ON HIS CARDINAL DUTIES

This requires the ability to discriminate between what he alone must do and what can be done by subordinates—or neglected. Then he sticks to his job. Concentrating on central issues inevitably confronts him with decision-making—hard, repellent, risky work that sometimes tempts him to wander back to the fascinating details of some earlier work. But he forces himself to avoid preoccupation with irrelevant trifles.

HE HAS A SENSE OF HUMOR

Knowing that he is only human and, therefore, subject to all the human frailties—vanity, pomposity, self-importance—he is smart enough never to take himself too seriously. He knows, too, that a laugh is one of the healthiest ways to relieve the day-to-day pressures under which he inevitably works. And he recognizes that without laughter, all the rest—the authority, the importance, the work itself—isn't worth very much.

HE MAKES HIS PEOPLE WANT TO PERFORM WELL

Fully realizing that people do things for a driver when they are *forced* to do them and that they do their jobs enthusiastically for a leader because he makes them *want* to follow his wishes, he has mastered a variety of strategies designed to motivate employees to do their best.

Here are five such strategies that you can adapt to your own needs.

PRACTICE EFFECTIVE HUMAN RELATIONS

The first requirement in practicing good human relations is to recognize the broad needs of your employees, not purely from a "do-good" point of view but as enlightened self-interest. If you recognize that it takes more than a full pay envelope to make a contented employee and if you resolve to try to fill his other needs by running your department or company along sound human relations principles, then half your battle is won.

An effective human relations program requires an understanding of the varied feelings, hopes, fears and values of your employees. On the one hand, it means personal interest in the individual worker. On the other hand, it does *not* mean paternalism, pampering and neglect of discipline. As boss, your problem is to fit together the logical conduct of your operations and the emotional characteristics of your employees as individuals. To do this successfully calls for knowing how to work with people both individually and in groups.

There is no single formula for sound employee relations. Quite aside from a decent salary, there are certain things that almost all people, in varying degrees, want from their jobs.

Most employees, for example, have a keen desire for challenging work, an opportunity to use *all* their talents. Give them assignments that not only permit them to realize this ambition, but require that they "stretch" themselves and, perhaps, discover strengths that they had no idea they possessed and you will have gone a long way toward establishing the special man-manager rapport that pervades the most successful business organizations.

They crave an opportunity for advancement. They want to feel that when a better job opportunity opens up, they will be given a fair chance at it. People vary greatly in ambition and desire to get ahead, certainly; but your most valuable employees are likely to require that their jobs help them to grow as individuals. Promotions and other management support for advancement is one vital way in which to satisfy this need.

They also need a sense of security. They want to know that their jobs will still be there tomorrow, next week, next month, next year. Above all, they yearn to feel psychologically secure within the group in which they work. They want to accept their fellow workers and be fully accepted by them and their manager.

Effective leadership is important to them. They want to feel confident that their boss knows what he's doing, knows how to do it and is respected by others. They want to feel that the "steering wheel" on which their security and well-being depend is in good hands.

High in their hierarchy of needs, too, is a sense of participation. They want to feel that they are a part of the team, not just hired hands.

Finally, a healthy work environment is important to them. To as great a degree as your operations will permit, they want a safe, clean, well-lighted, and well-ventilated place in which to work, with good equipment. Moreover, depending on the situation, they may want parking facilities, snack bar, soft drink vending machines, and other employee services.

Here is an employee relations situation that was not well thought out: one company president decided that the men in his plant were starved for color, so he had the grounds seeded with grass. When it began growing lushly, he had flower boxes planted with geraniums and placed under the plant windows.

"That should be the finishing touch," he thought with satisfaction. The very next day his workers struck. One of them was heard to mutter, "Those damn geraniums are the last straw!"

The poor president was amazed. "How ungrateful can workers be?" he wondered. What he had not thought of, or bothered to find out, was that the men had been accustomed to sitting out in the yard to have their lunch. Now they were confronted with a sign telling them to keep off the grass!

Don't make the mistake of giving your employees what *you* think they want or what *you* think would be good for them. If you are planning improvements of any worth in your employee facilities, find out first what they *really* want. They will repay you with good work.

Here are some additional human relations practices that can help you win cooperation from your subordinates. You undoubtedly do many of these things already, but even if you spot only one or two areas that you may have been neglecting and make them part of your regular routine, your performance —and theirs—should improve noticeably.

SHOW INTEREST IN THEM

Some years ago, the Western Electric Company conducted an experiment that revolutionized management thinking.

The objective was to determine whether better lighting would increase production. Two groups of workers were selected for observation. Group A worked under the same illumination at all times; Group B worked under varying lighting conditions. As expected, production rose as brightness of illumination increased.

But what was *not* expected was this: the production of Group A, working under the old lighting conditions, also rose!

The engineers reversed the procedure. Instead of increasing the amount of available light, they decreased it. From 10 foot-candles they dropped it to nine, then eight, then seven. Production still didn't fall off!

When they reached three foot-candles, workers complained and the experiments were discontinued. But two volunteers continued to work under the ever-diminishing light. At 0.06 foot-candles of light—*the equivalent of ordinary moonlight* —they maintained their customary efficiency. They reported feeling less tired at the end of a day's work than before the experiments began and no eyestrain whatever.

After endless checking, only one conclusion was possible. Simply by conducting the experiment, the company had showed its workers how interested it was in each of them. By watching them, asking them questions and generally fussing over them, Western Electric had made its employees feel like individuals instead of mere cogs in an industrial machine.

The moral is clear: *people work better when they feel that someone is taking an interest in them.*

DON'T OVERLOOK THE IMPORTANCE OF "PSYCHIC INCOME"

Most managers think that they are sufficiently compensating their subordinates if their take-home pay compares favorably with that of peers in other firms. But more and more companies are discovering that workers want—indeed, crave—other forms of "pay." Here are the most important kinds of non-monetary compensation that help keep employees satisfied:

RESPONSIBILITY. You can pay a king's ransom in wages, but if he is not allowed to make decisions, he may get unhappy and quit.

PRIVILEGES. Special prerogatives, ranging from preferred parking to a painting on his office wall, go a long way toward convincing a man that his unique contribution to the firm is appreciated.

INSIDE INFORMATION. Part of a worker's "psychic income" is inspiration. The best way to inspire him is to let him in on the show—your dreams, hopes, plans. If you let your people share all the satisfactions that business gives, they will work all the harder.

RECOGNITION. A public pat on the back, a symbolic reward for special achievement (*e.g.*, inclusion in an honor list, a name plate, medal, cup, plaque), even a personalized joke can go a long way toward adding to the enjoyment he derives from doing his best.

KEEP YOUR STANDARDS CONSISTENT

When a man knows he is being judged by a single, fair standard, he has a target to aim for. He can modify his performance accordingly and try to meet that standard. No one wants to, or can, work without an objective. To be consistent to the point of inflexibility, however, is poor management. But if you are going to modify your standards, at least communicate this in advance so that your people can expect a measure of flexibility and remain flexible themselves.

ALLOW FREEDOM OF EXPRESSION

Assuming that your people are reasonably competent, it never hurts to relax your vigil and allow them to do things *their* way once in a while. Every employee ought to have the right to make his own job more interesting by doing it his way. All you have to do is be sure that the results are what you seek and that the employee is working within the framework of company policy. Experiments have shown that, even on assembly-line operations, this technique works. Girls who are given some discretion, for instance, as to what time to take their coffee breaks are more highly motivated than when the coffee break times are simply posted. A salesman who schedules his road trips himself is likely to work harder, see more customers in less time, than when he receives a schedule from the home office.

BE WILLING TO ASSUME THE RESPONSIBILITY FOR YOUR PEOPLE

If you want to get things done through people, you must assume some responsibility for what they do. The employee who doesn't feel that he has the backing of his boss is not apt to stick his neck out with new ideas, bold solutions or unorthodox methods—lest he have his head chopped off. But the employee who *knows* that he has the backing of his superior can employ his full energies to doing his job in the best way he knows how.

HOLD WEEKLY CONFERENCES

People like to be let in on things, to see how their efforts are related to company goals and achievements. Toward this end, call your people together periodically (on Monday mornings, say) for a 10- or 15-minute meeting at which time work requirements for the forthcoming week are discussed. This is the time to encourage reports on problems or work difficulties encountered and to comment on new developments in store for the immediate future. This is also a good time for handing out well-deserved compliments. Never regard your meeting as a mere "get-together"; plan it in advance, with an agenda, so that it is a constructive, informative session.

MAKE THEM PROUD OF THEIR JOBS

No matter what he does, every employee wants to take pride in his job. The desire for the approval of others that is built into all human beings is a powerful incentive to which every employee will respond.

During World War II, for example, one of the least heralded, dirtiest—but most essential—jobs in our shipyards was that of the scaler. His job was to chip the rust off steel plates on prefabricated sections. He worked in a confined double bottom, a space no larger than a three-foot high passenger elevator, if you can imagine such a thing. The noise was unrelentingly deafening. Rust dust permeated the air he breathed. And only inches above him were steel plates upon which beat the blazing sun.

The scalers in one large western shipyard, aware of the toughness of their job, resented the fact that they were not being paid journeyman wages for it. Their mounting anger finally manifested itself in a slowdown.

One young scaler was offered—and accepted—the job of foreman over several hundred of his co-workers, a job that many experienced foremen had turned down. Immediately, he began visiting his men. He agreed that they were doing the dirtiest, unhealthiest, least heralded job there was in a shipyard. Furthermore, it was an obvious injustice that journeyman pay was not mentioned in the union contract by which they were compelled to abide.

"But," he pointed out, "your job, bad as it is, is a crucial one. That rust has to be removed. Wherever you go in this yard, the other workers see your scaler buttons and they know you have what it takes. Deep down, they also know that they couldn't do what you're doing."

With renewed pride in their jobs, the scalers abandoned the slowdown and returned to work, carrying their heads a little higher than usual. And all because the young foreman instinctively recognized the importance of instilling in them pride in their work.

THROW DOWN A CHALLENGE

Long before income taxes, when a dollar in salary meant a dollar in your pocket, one of the biggest wage earners in the world was Charles Schwab, the steel magnate. Andrew Carnegie cheerfully paid him a salary of *one million dollars a year*.

Yet Schwab was no great financial wizard. Nor was he especially knowledgeable in the field of steel fabrication.

What, then, made him worth *$3,000 a day* to the Carnegie Steel Corporation?

Andrew Carnegie answered that question when he said, "Charlie has a positive genius for handling men."

Perhaps the most illuminating example of that genius in action occurred when Schwab was confronted by the problem of a mill with a particularly poor record of production. He talked the problem over with the mill manager and asked bluntly, "Why are your men falling so far below their quotas?"

"I honestly don't know," the manager replied. "I've tried every trick in the book with them. I've coaxed them; I've pleaded with them; I've threatened them; I've cussed them. But nothing works. They're hopeless."

"Get me a piece of chalk and meet me over there," Schwab said, indicating a knot of workmen.

When he had the chalk, Schwab asked one of the workers, "How many heats did your shift make today?"

"Six," the man told him.

Schwab bent down, chalked a large 6 on the floor and walked away.

When the night shift reported for work, they were curious about the number on the floor. What did it mean?

The day workers explained.

On the following morning, Schwab dropped in at the mill again. But his 6 had disappeared. In its place was a large 7, put there by the night shift.

The day shift rose to the challenge. By the time they quit work, they were able to erase the 7 and replace it with a bold 8. The night shift responded with a gigantic 9. The day shift countered with a swaggering 11. In no time at all, the mill that had been "hopeless" was transformed into the company's top producer.

"One of the easiest ways to get things done," Schwab explained to the mill manager, "is to stimulate friendly rivalry. I don't mean in a money-getting way, but in the desire to excel."

Try it yourself. When other methods fail, throw down a challenge. The vast majority of employees will respond enthusiastically.

CREATE SOME PURPOSEFUL TENSION

The challenge is only one way of attacking employee lethargy, but it suggests a whole strategy of motivation that is rarely utilized: the creation of tension.

Contrary to common opinion, a reasonable amount of anxiety is not bad for employees. In fact, it can be a tonic, for psychological tension keeps men from growing complacent and set in their ways. It shakes them up mentally, heightening attention, facilitating learning and improving performance. Furthermore, a reasonable amount of tension provides interest and excitement for people. Result: ambition and achievement rise. From personal experience, you can undoubtedly recall many instances of far surpassing your own expectations of yourself when the chips were down and you had to perform under pressure.

Creating tension to inspire better performance is as old as the threat of dismissal, to be sure, but there are subtler spurs to improvement available to you. Here are some alternatives to consider.

ESTABLISH DEADLINES

Firm, fixed deadlines compel an employee to plan his work. They also help overcome the temptation to procrastinate that is built into any assignment given on a "When-you-have-a-chance" basis.

There are at least three good reasons for setting deadlines.

First, you challenge the worker with them. Everyone cherishes a certain image of himself and will do anything to sustain it. Almost everyone's idealized portrait of himself includes a sense of honor. We like to believe we can be counted on. By establishing a time limit in which to accomplish something, you are challenging your employee's good opinion of himself. In order to meet that challenge, he will summon all his capabilities. This "face saving" is an enormous incentive.

Second, you are being affirmative. "If you think you can,

you can," it's been said. That may be restated, "If you think your subordinate can, he'll try like blazes." If you tell an employee, "We'll want that report ready for Tuesday's nine o'clock conference," you're really declaring your belief in his ability to deliver by the stated time. It's always easier to do something if you know somebody else is sure you can do it. Positive thinking, to a degree, *is* contagious.

Third, you alert his body. By establishing a deadline, you trigger a physiological chain of events that makes accomplishment easier for your subordinate, for the knowledge that a certain task must be completed by a specified time alerts the body to prepare itself for the job at hand. If the work is physical, muscles flex and tighten; breathing increases to deliver extra oxygen; the pulse quickens as the heart pumps more blood to all parts of the body. Many other subtle physical changes take place. Even if the assignment is primarily mental, the body responds by sending more blood—and oxygen—to the brain.

A word of advice: keep your deadlines challenging but realistic. Make them too tough and you will only discourage your subordinates.

SET QUOTAS

Long used in sales, quotas are beginning to be recognized in other departments for the effective motivators that they are. Quotas, of course, are designed to give a man a specific goal to aim at.

Ask a man to come up with "some solutions" to a problem, for example, and you may get two or three. But ask him to prepare half a dozen options from which you can choose and you will get your six solutions. If necessary, make him "reach out" for the answers—to other departments, other people, out-of-the-ordinary places.

This type of challenge can be particularly useful in the case of a man who seldom communicates with outsiders. Your quota may compel him to get out of his rut, encourage the cross-pollination of ideas. He and you can only benefit from the experience.

USE RIDICULE

A salesman recoils at the prospect of calling on a tough customer. You shame him into it by using the "Are you a man or a mouse?" approach.

A supervisor writes off a worker as hopeless—he's tardy, sullen, uncooperative. You challenge the supervisor's ingenuity with, "If we only had perfect workers, we wouldn't need you, would we, Frank?"

Your assistant throws in the towel after only one try at an assignment. "Don't tell me you've exhausted all 10 billion brain cells already!" you shout in mock surprise.

There are times when appealing to a man's fighting instincts by ridiculing or shaming him is the best way to get through to him. Sure, you run the risk of temporarily losing a friend, but in the long run you will gain an effective employee.

It goes without saying that this technique should be used in private only. Keep it on a man-to-man basis, so that the employee has only to prove himself to two people: you and himself.

"CREATE" EMERGENCIES

Most people don't know what they are really capable of doing for a very simple reason: they've never had an opportunity to test themselves. Used to occupying a certain position in the highly stratified society of a company, they know that their area of responsibility covers only cases D through F. Situation B? That's Jones' department. Emergency G? That's Smith's problem.

You can broaden their horizons, increase their self-reliance and revitalize them by purposely throwing hot potatoes into their laps on occasion. Want to "stretch" an assistant? Take off for a day or two on short notice, leaving him in charge. Reshuffle vacation schedules, forcing new responsibilities on your staff. Take the desk-bound man along with you on your next business trip as an adviser.

What's in it for you? Employees who have renewed faith

in their own abilities and are again excited about their jobs, their company and themselves.

GIVE THEM RECOGNITION

Every man enjoys a pat on the back. It proves that his contribution to his company, and society, is recognized and appreciated. It shows that he is more than just a faceless member of a large group. And it confirms his own belief in his worth as a human being.

In short, praise is a valuable technique of motivation because a healthy egotism is an important part of the average person's psychic make-up. Who isn't buoyed up by a compliment? A little flattery, even when its sincerity is mildly suspect, makes our day. And because we tend to live up to the image that others have of us, most of us will do everything in our power not to disappoint those who praise us.

Nor is it all that difficult to find something to compliment in another human being. "You handled that customer beautifully" . . . "That's a bright idea" . . . "We appreciate the long hours you've been putting in"—these are just a few of the bouquets it is no great strain to pass out.

Yet, many managers find this difficult to do. Sometimes, it is because they are so full of self-confidence themselves that they require no outside assurances of their ability. Assuming that others are like them, they see no reason to compliment subordinates. Occasionally, they are simply insensitive to the needs of others. Or, they are so riddled with self-doubt themselves that they cannot believe that their opinion of others really matters.

In any case, it is the subordinates who suffer. Not getting the credit they deserve, they are apt to think, "Why try?" Result: morale—and efficiency—plunge.

PUT WHAT YOU WANT DONE
IN TERMS OF THEIR OWN SELF–INTEREST

Ninety-two percent of the average person's thinking time, psychologists tell us, is spent in thinking about—himself!

Why not take advantage of this human quirk? Explain what you want done in terms that are virtually guaranteed to trigger enthusiasm—*self-interest.*

Some examples of this technique in action:

"By getting that report finished on time, you'll make yourself available for a bigger job."

"I know the men in the front office will be proud of you when they hear you've identified our production bottleneck."

"You won't risk injury if you wear these special gloves whenever you operate this machine."

Before giving an order or issuing instructions, ask yourself what benefit or advantage your employee can anticipate if he accomplishes what you want. Then "translate" your order into these "what's-in-it-for-him" terms.

Childish? Immature?

Maybe. Maybe not.

One thing is sure—it works.

In business, that's usually what counts.

Chapter Ten

Managing
for Better Morale

You can't see it, touch it or measure it. Yet, if it isn't present in a company, you can tell soon enough. People work side by side, but not together. Jobs get done, but without enthusiasm or excellence. Pride in performance is virtually nonexistent.

It's morale, the invisible cement that binds men together and permits their combined achievements somehow to add up to more than the sum of their individual efforts.

When people describe a firm as enjoying high morale, they don't necessarily mean that everyone is on a first name, "buddy" basis. You can find top-drawer morale in companies where the boss is always "Mister" or "sir." Nor is high morale invariably the result of placid, low-pressure conditions; in fact, studies indicate that such an atmosphere can actually cause *low* morale. Getting the work out in any firm facing tough competition—and that includes just about every company these days—is more than just a game. It is a serious job calling for team effort and discipline, both of which flourish best in an atmosphere of *esprit de corps.*

Morale might be called the spirit of a company—the sum total of the attitudes of its people. It is influenced more from the top down than from the bottom up. It is often more a matter of how the boss says "Good morning" than of whether or not people work without neckties. No single condition will consistently explain good or poor morale, for it is a "mix" of many related elements operating together in a company at any given time.

At the outset you should understand that your personal ways of interpreting your people's actions and conversations may lead to false conclusions about the state of their morale. Some of the factors affecting morale are clear, but others are not. Contrary to popular opinion, there are usually many kinds of reasons behind an employee's feelings. Generally speaking, you can divide them into four categories:

1. Reasons an employee can talk about freely and objectively;
2. Reasons he talks about readily enough, but which actually are distortions of fact;
3. Reasons he doesn't want to discuss because he is sensitive about them; and
4. Reasons he is unable to talk about because he himself doesn't know they exist.

Reasons 2, 3 and 4 are likely to be characterized by a high emotional content. The trouble is that most employees do not easily recognize and express the less logical reasons behind their feelings. Consequently, it becomes particularly important for the boss to be aware of them. If he is, he will be more inclined to act on the basis of those significant underlying feelings which most affect morale. Very often, the stated reasons for dissatisfaction are not the real ones.

WHAT GOES INTO GOOD MORALE?

This question brings up two points. First, certain basic needs are shared by all people: food, shelter, safety and acceptance. Second, the ways in which these needs can be satisfied in individual cases depends on such factors as education, previous experience, social relationships and age, for morale means different things to different people. There is no one need which is always Number 1 for *all* workers.

Thus, different groups tend to emphasize different factors. Lower and middle income groups, for example, attach great importance to security. White-collar groups, on the other hand, tend to rate such factors as opportunity for self-expression, independence and interesting work as most significant. Those in higher income brackets give greater weight to status and social approval.

From the standpoint of the job itself, research has identified some 14 factors as important in building morale. This, of course, is only one breakdown; there are many others. Moreover, since they cover both sexes and all age ranges, *all* may not be applicable to any one age or sex. Yet, despite limitations, it is a very useful series. In descending order of their significance, then, the 14 are:

1. Security
2. Interest
3. Opportunity for advancement
4. Appreciation
5. Company and management
6. Intrinsic aspects of job assignment
7. Wages
8. Supervision
9. Social aspects of job
10. Working conditions
11. Communication
12. Hours
13. Ease
14. Benefits

Many people put great stress on the importance of money in morale. But notice: wages rank half way down the list and benefits finish dead last. The fact is that financial incentives alone are *not* enough to produce top level morale. Once an employee's basic needs are satisfied through *adequate* pay, other non-monetary aspects of the job take on ever-increasing significance. To be sure, people often say that wages are the reason for their taking extreme action. But investigation indicates that lack of fulfillment of other less obvious, less rational needs is actually the prime cause in many cases.

For example, the quality of supervision is often a major factor in morale. Not surprisingly, employee-oriented executives and supervisors usually get the best results from their people. The employee who feels he is wanted and needed as a human being is more favorably disposed toward his boss than the employee who feels he represents only another body to his manager. Consequently, the first employee's morale is higher and, in all probability, he does a better job than his less valued counterpart.

Dirty wash rooms have been the basis for strikes. Granting bonuses instead of modest pay increases has led to slowdowns. In at least one case, the building of partitions between certain job areas could have prevented labor strife.

Such instances should be seen in terms of emotional needs. When those needs are left unfulfilled, there is frustration. Morale dips. And if morale goes down far enough, people do something about it.

That's why it pays to watch closely for "unimportant" and "illogical" factors which influence morale as well as for such generally recognized factors as working conditions. Complaints about them may actually cover up far more significant problems, like fear of future change.

HOW GOOD IS MORALE IN YOUR FIRM TODAY?

To answer that question, you must watch for events that prevent employee needs from being filled. Examples are common. Take the case of the manager who contributes to poor morale by failing to investigate and scotch a false rumor that his department is going to be eliminated. Or consider another executive who keeps all information about the business to himself. He wants to keep his competitors guessing, but he only hurts morale in his own firm in the process.

Recognize too that the varied groups in your organization

—executives, supervisors, employees, part-time seasonal help and so on—do not share the same goals. Note the degree to which they overlap (or fail to overlap) the company's goals. For instance, secretary Mary Jones wants very much to get married. She wants a spot where she can be with and meet eligible young men. Management, on the other hand, has a different goal—getting out correspondence. As a result, it assigns her where its need is greatest, which happens to be in a back room. Then it wonders why her morale is low.

Against this background, try to spot first of all the symptoms which indicate the level of morale. High employee turnover, absenteeism, grievances, complaints and the like tend to go with poor morale. The same holds true for long faces, short tempers, hot arguments and cold silences. The opposite conditions usually reflect good morale.

So take an objective look at your area of responsibility, be it a single department, a division or an entire company. As the boss, you may find this hard to do. You may, in fact, want to get some outside assistance. However it is done, a comprehensive procedure in evaluating present morale will include these steps:

1. Size up the overall "personality" of your department of company;
2. Watch for ups and downs in morale;
3. Check with your key subordinates to see how well *their* thinking conforms to *your* goals;
4. Get objective views from your employees regarding the important factors in morale; and finally,
5. Go after supplementary information on matters of special importance in your particular operation.

To be sure, these are broad steps. Specific techniques vary from company to company. Most of them involve some type of interviewing and various sorts of anonymous questionnaires. As a practical matter, however, standardized surveys and related devices which are widely available can be put to good use no matter what the size of your organization. Note, also, the value of getting employee participation. Get your employees' help in suggesting changes and putting them into effect. Too often the boss gets into trouble for one reason: forgetting that his employees are the world's greatest authorities on what they want, he decides, all by himself, what changes are needed to improve morale. And, of course, as often as not he goofs.

The things employees say they object to are often not the real problems. This condition stems from the fact that most people tend to express dissatisfaction only in concrete terms. They get upset when they are "not paid fairly" or are "treated like children" or are "kept under somebody's thumb." But emotions are abstract. They are much more difficult to put into words than salary or wages. Thus, a complaint about wages may actually disguise a man's deeper feeling that the boss is sore at him. In reality, of course, the boss may not be angry at all, but he may have done or said something which made the employee think he was.

Unless you identify the real causes of poor morale, you may well go to work on the wrong problem. In determining the true state of morale in your organization, you can get assistance quite readily and reasonably from professional psychologists associated with local universities or consulting organizations.

HOW TO IMPROVE EMPLOYEE MORALE

No simple, guaranteed ground rules for improving employee morale can be established, for every situation is unique. No two individuals are exactly alike, nor are any two companies identical. Nevertheless, from psychological research on morale and attitudes in business, certain practical suggestions may be made.

Demonstrate to your employees that you are genuinely interested in them and would be glad to have their ideas on how conditions might be improved.

Treat your employees as individuals; never deal with them as impersonal variables in a working unit.

Accept the fact that others may not see things as you do.

Respect differences of opinion.

Insofar as possible, give explanations for management actions.

Provide information and guidance on matters affecting employees' security.

Make reasonable efforts to keep jobs interesting—by occasionally adding new responsibilities, new challenges, new authority.

Encourage promotion from within.

Express appreciation publicly for jobs well done.

Offer criticism privately in the form of constructive suggestions for improvement.

Train supervisors to think about the people involved insofar as practicable, rather than just the work.

Keep your people up-to-date on all business matters affecting them and quell rumors with correct information.

Be fair.

BUILDING EXECUTIVE MORALE

Executives have emotional needs, frustrations and good or poor morale, too, just like other employees. The above suggestions for improving employee morale are generally applicable to supervisors and executives. In addition, however, some further ideas are appropriate to this latter group.

Actually, they are more a matter of emphasis than of new information.

Take your key man or men into your confidence; let people work *with* you rather than just *for* you.

Encourage mutual cooperation as well as individualism.

Obtain agreement on the goals of your company.

Educate your management group (even if it's only two or three people) to the goals of the company.

Keep your managerial team informed of your plans and activities.

Make lines of responsibility and authority clear.

Specify the nature of relationships among executives—upper, lower and equal levels.

Give your executives clear-cut decisions.

See that their privileges and office facilities are in keeping with their status.

Provide equitable compensation.

RECAP

Accidents, turnover, absenteeism and grievances tend to be more common where morale is low. Productivity, efficiency and customer relations also suffer where negative attitudes exist. As the boss, don't overlook the personal satisfaction—and extra profit—than comes with running an organization where *esprit de corps* is high.

DROP YOUR VALUED SUGGESTION HERE

WASTE

Chapter Eleven

Coming to Grips with Employee Gripes

They can take any of a hundred forms: "My manager dislikes me." "Nobody tells you what's going on around here." "The food in the cafeteria is a disgrace."

Every executive must expect to run into some employee griping. And, depending on his ability to handle them, they can be frustrating, costly experiences—or positively priceless opportunities to sew up an employee's allegiance.

Which they shall be is largely determined by five factors —the executive's

Skill in avoiding the most common grievance-handling pitfalls

Attitudes and approach

Capacity for "discovering the villain"

Ability to find solutions

Knack for cashing in on complaints

In that order.

AVOIDING THE PITFALLS

Handled correctly, a grievance can be a stimulant to more effective communications between man and manager, a healthy
safety valve that permits the griper to get things off his chest
and, consequently, obtain satisfaction. Mishandled or ignored,
even a minor complaint can mushroom into anger, and from
there follow a progression through stubbornness, spitefulness,
uncooperativeness and, finally, disloyalty. In dealing with other
people's dissatisfactions, executives are frequently guilty of in-
sensitivity and haste. Here are the more common blunders to
avoid:

1. KEEPING YOURSELF UNAVAILABLE

Of course you're a busy man. There are a multitude of demands on your time. There are meetings to attend, paperwork
to handle, plans to draw up, superiors to report to, work to over-
see. Under such circumstances, an individual employee's grievance can seem very insignificant. But bear in mind that to the
worker it is of paramount importance. If he cannot turn to you
for satisfaction, to whom can he go? Deny him the one logical
outlet in your organization for what is bothering him and you
are setting the stage for massive discontent. So make yourself
available.

2. NOT GIVING HIM YOUR UNDIVIDED ATTENTION

It is not enough to allow the employee to tell you his story.
You must give him your complete attention. It is insulting to
invite a man to talk to you, then riffle through papers, take telephone calls or walk around while he is unburdening himself.

3. NOT TAKING THE COMPLAINT SERIOUSLY

Shaking your head, clucking your tongue, smiling in an all-
knowing manner while a worker is relating his problem to you

—these are only a few of the ways you can tell him that you think his complaint lacks merit. Remember that the overwhelming majority of employees will not come to you unless they are convinced that their cases are just. And if one of your people feels strongly enough to articulate a grievance, then you owe him the courtesy of a serious, attentive hearing.

4. EXPRESSING AN OPINION TOO SOON

To reach a conclusion before you have all the evidence is not only manifestly unfair; by so doing, you risk appearing ignorant to your subordinates. And once your people lose respect for you, your ability to manage effectively is irreparably damaged.

5. STOPPING TOO SOON IN THE SEARCH FOR FACTS

Go after the reasons for a complaint with too little curiosity or tenacity and you are apt to give subordinates the impression that you want to prove them wrong. As a manager, your primary interest should be in the truth behind a grievance. Toward that end, be unsparing in your efforts to uncover the facts. Talk to other people when necessary. Look up documentation. Ask your own superiors for interpretations of policies. But get the facts.

6. PROCRASTINATING

Since nothing is more important to a successful organization than its people, you attack the very foundation of your company when you do anything that depresses employee morale and, as a result, performance. Drag your heels in responding to a complaint and you are tacitly announcing to the complainer that you don't consider his grievance (and, by inference, him) very important. How long do you think he'll remain loyal to the company or care to work hard on its behalf?

7. HIDING BEHIND RED TAPE

"I'll have to check that out with Personnel." "As soon as I get the proper forms to fill out, I'll pass your complaint along." "You'll have to go through channels." The manager who puts off an employee's gripe by appealing to bureaucracy may succeed in temporarily stifling the complaint, but at the same time he is laying the foundation for another, larger beef.

8. NOT LETTING AN EMPLOYEE KNOW WHAT'S BEING DONE ABOUT HIS COMPLAINT

Because an employee's complaint is just one of many items on his calendar, a manager may neglect to keep a man informed of its disposition. But just as we can only think of the one tooth that aches, so an employee dwells on the subject of his discontent. "No man's affairs, however small, are unimportant to him," said Lord Acton—a truism every executive might well ponder.

9. NOT CHECKING ON THE SETTLEMENT OF A COMPLAINT

Grievances are seldom pleasant things. Perhaps that's why some managers are eager to drop them as soon as possible. A crucial final step, however, is to see that a complaint is resolved —by removing the cause of it, compensating for it in some way or proving, to the employee's satisfaction, that his complaint was unwarranted. Like any other job, in short, a grievance should be seen through to the end.

10. NOT FORGETTING A GRIEVANCE ONCE IT IS RESOLVED

When we bear a grudge, we bear the heaviest, most profitless burden of all, for it consumes valuable energy better spent in other activities, it poisons relationships and it undermines the very essence of teamwork. Unfortunately, it is all too human to remember complaints, particularly if we figure in them. But dwelling on the past accomplishes little. And, as a manager, one of your main concerns is necessarily with accomplishment.

So, in the matter of employee grievances, resolve that once a case is closed, it is closed forever. Your people will respect you for it.

So much for the "don'ts" of handling complaints. Let us now turn our attention to the "do's."

ATTITUDE AND APPROACH

The knowledgeable executive sees a gripe for what it really is— a chance to be of help to an employee when that help is most wanted, a golden opportunity to prove to a worker that his problem is management's problem.

But you can't expect an employee to believe you care unless you show him that you do. This means, first of all, *taking the complaint seriously.* Whether your employee thinks you're giving him the evil eye or grumbles about poor leadership is immaterial. As far as he's concerned, he has a legitimate beef. Minimize it in any way and you immediately compound his grievance because you are, in effect, challenging his judgment.

Recognize, therefore, that when a man comes to you with a complaint, it probably represents weeks, even months, of gnawing doubt, discomfort, and anxiety. Resist the temptation to belittle it, no matter how farfetched or baseless it may be. Remember that, as an executive, you enjoy a larger view of things—a view that permits you to see events in a grander context with more perspective. Lacking this wider view, the employee may very well be suffering from tunnel vision, but it isn't his fault. It is woven into the very fabric of the corporate structure. In short, be understanding.

This becomes particularly important when you consider that a man with a gripe is in no mood to be reasonable. Not at first. Above all, he craves an audience, someone to whom he can pour out his tale of woe. Therefore, the smart manager makes it a point, at the first hint of trouble, to *establish communications with the dissatisfied employee.* If it isn't possible to arrange for an immediate face-to-face confrontation, make an appointment for the near future. It's the very best way to show that you value his well-being and loyalty.

Once you are together, *listen.* Look interested. Display concern. Get all the facts. Don't speak until you are certain he has nothing more to say.

There is a very sound reason for this strategy.

Every automobile company maintains a customer relations staff whose sole job is to soothe the ruffled feathers of irate customers. Usually, a car owner is so burned up over his real or imagined grievances that the C.R. man serves as little more than a verbal punching bag—at first. By the time 99 out of 100 interviews—or telephone calls—end, however, the customer is completely satisfied, a loyal fan of the firm.

How do the C.R. men do it?

"Mostly," explains one, "we listen. Sometimes it's just to a lot of nonsense; sometimes, it's to a legitimate gripe. But no matter which classification a complaint falls under, it gets the same treatment—a cordial, sympathetic hearing. When the customer has a beef, most of all he wants an audience. After he's convinced that we know where he stands, he's willing to hear our side. Most important of all, we've learned through long experience, is that a talked-out griper is the easiest kind to deal with."

That's so important, it bears repeating: *a talked-out griper is the easiest to deal with.*

Remember that.

Having gotten a man's beef out in the open, you are ready to *summarize,* in your own words, his net valid complaint. This serves two purposes: it disarms the complainer by showing him how closely you have followed what he's been saying. And it helps you keep his points straight in your own mind.

Next to letting off steam, what the disgruntled employee wants most is satisfaction. If his complaint is justified, be quick to admit it—but be sure to explain *why* things went wrong and *why* a recurrence is all but impossible. Otherwise, your assurance that "It won't happen again" may sound like a hollow promise.

In short, welcome gripes as voluntary tip-offs to what you

can do to cement relations with your employees. It's the man with the silently nursed dissatisfaction who should worry you, for you'll never know how you can be of maximum help to him. The most skillful physician in the world cannot treat a patient who refuses to tell him where it hurts.

"DISCOVERING THE VILLAIN"

One of the biggest mistakes a manager can make in handling a gripe is to pin the blame on "someone in the front office." Passing the buck can only arouse suspicions, as if the manager were saying, "It's not my fault, but I'll help you anyway." Rather than dig for excuses, ask the employee, "What happened?" That way, you boil the whole issue down to *what* went wrong rather than *who* is to blame. You ally yourself with him in a search for the common enemy—the cause of his complaint. When you find it, get rid of it if you can.

Sometimes, the grievance is based on simple error. When that's the case, a calm review of the circumstances may divulge the culprit.

The personnel director of a large appliance manufacturing firm cites the production line employee who inexplicably began grumbling about the poor conditions under which they had to work. The ventilation was suddenly poor. Lighting, they claimed, was inadequate. The food in the vending machines was indigestible. The noise from the machinery was frazzling their nerves. Just about everything in their working environment was subjected to a steady barrage of criticism.

Since they had never complained before so vociferously and unanimously about so many things at once, an investigation was held. As it turned out, their griping was *really* caused by the gnawing suspicion that they were soon to be the victims of automation. With no prior warning, management had invited a leasing firm (to whom they were considering selling their plant, then leasing it back) to inspect the factory. The sudden appearance of unidentified snoopers had triggered employee suspicions; the rumor mill had done the rest. Once the leasing executives were satisfactorily explained, employee complaints about poor working conditions evaporated like magic.

While all gripes are not so easily settled, many do fall under certain broad categories. Next time you find yourself facing a grumbling employee, consider these possibilities. They *could* save you from a lot of sound and fury.

MISUNDERSTANDING

A lot of gripes are based on simple lack of information. The employee who doesn't get as long a vacation as another because he hasn't been with the firm long enough—the man who misreads your explanation of certain fringe benefits—the worker whose tax refund has not lived up to expectations because of new government policy—each is basing his dissatisfaction on a different frame of reference from you. Such "emotional static" can lead to a verbal free-for-all. A few well-placed questions and some patient answers can clear the air.

TRANSFERRED ANGER

Employees, remember, are also husbands, wives, parents, consumers, in-laws, neighbors, taxpayers, citizens, and many other things. The man who comes to work fresh from a quarrel with his wife, or who lost more than he should have at his weekly poker game, or who is being dunned by his creditors will often transfer his frustration and anger to the people among whom—or the conditions under which—he works. The woman who complains about poor rest room accommodations at her place of employment may really be striking back at what she considers a social affront experienced over the weekend.

A few tactful questions about how things are going at home can frequently uncover the true villain.

POOR COMMUNICATIONS

Your instructions to an employee may seem crystal clear—*to you*. But they may be Greek to the person to whom they are addressed. Result: a badly done job and a guilt-ridden employee who may gripe in anticipation of being criticized.

Solution: make *very* sure, via repetition, questions, demonstrations, an "open-door" policy that encourages two-way communications, that employees fully understand what is expected of them.

IMPROPER DIAGNOSIS

A production worker complains about the performance of his machine. You investigate and find that faulty wiring is to blame. Your people grumble over the new working hours, are mollified when they are informed that the new work day is geared to help them avoid the day's worst traffic. An irate employee gripes about the new specifications for a job—until you point out that they come straight from the customer.

Sometimes, an outside factor, one you have nothing to do with, is the cause of the complaint. Find it if you can—and make a friend.

But suppose an employee's gripe is justified? What then?

FINDING SOLUTIONS

The main reason for investigating a gripe is to undo some kind of damage—to morale, performance or personal relationships.

Easier said than done?

Of course! But well within the executive's power—providing he learns how to find solutions that are mutually acceptable to the employee and his company.

The first step toward finding such solutions is to familiarize yourself with your company's facilities and policies. Precisely what are its agreements with any unions involved? What departments are especially equipped to help employees with offbeat problems (*e.g.,* some medical departments maintain resident psychiatrists, some firms offer interest-free loans to employees from a fund set aside for that express purpose)? How far does your own authority to work things out extend?

The answers to such questions will automatically set limits to the kind of redress you can offer your people—but the result will be *proposals that you know you can live up to.*

Once you know what you can do for an employee, tell him, precisely, concretely, honestly. If you cannot give him an immediate answer, tell him you will take it up with your firm and give him the answer within a few days. Then live up to your promise.

The second step toward finding mutually acceptable solutions is to ask your employee, after telling him what you will do about his complaint, "Is that acceptable to you?" Encourage his comments on the justice of your plan, for such encouragement pays a double dividend. It indicates your confidence in the fairness of the proposal and it proves your interest in eliminating the cause of his grievance.

Employees are generally reasonable. What they want—and have a right to expect—is fair play. Erase the *cause* of a complaint and, in 9 cases out of 10, you will hear no more about it. But it's a good idea to take the initiative later and check back on the situation.

CASHING IN ON COMPLAINTS

It is one thing to "take care" of a gripe, quite another to turn it to advantage. Yet, it's done every day, in a wide variety of ways. Here are the most important ones.

1. SELF-IMPROVEMENT

In those cases in which a manager is personally at fault, a gripe can be a blessing in disguise. For example, if investigation shows that employee morale is poor because the manager neglected to explain some new company policy clearly, he can take steps to clarify his future communications. Even if a personality quirk is alienating workers, he can work on eliminating the cause of the friction. The important thing is to look on every form of criticism—including employee grievances—as a spring-board to better performance.

2. COMPANY FEED-BACK

If a particular kind of gripe becomes common among your employees and investigation bears this out, possibly some company procedure or practice requires change. In the case of such legitimate complaints, examine the possibility of eliminating this cause by bringing them to the attention of your firm's policy makers. Or, if *you* are the "man with the muscle," consider changing things. Anything you can do to improve employee morale—and, as a result, productivity—is bound to improve your own position.

3. YOUR OTHER EMPLOYEES

A wholesaler who had always enjoyed cordial relations with his employees was surprised to hear from one of his senior workers that the firm's parking facilities were unsatisfactory. A quick check indicated that the complaint had merit. Over the years, the company had grown considerably and parking spaces had been added accordingly. However, parking was on a first-come, first-served basis and the last parking spaces were located a good 3–4 blocks away from the firm's entrance. The hike to work from car to entrance was particularly uncomfortable during the winter months.

The wholesaler immediately had a dozen of the closest parking spaces earmarked for those employees longest with the firm. The rest were numbered and the other employees were issued numbers monthly, rotating the most and least desirable spaces. Result: 120 employees impressed by the firm's desire to keep them happy.

The moral? Worker A's gripe could be an anticipation of B's, C's and D's. After checking out A's, why not change things if justified and show yourself off as a *voluntary* trouble-shooter? Neat. Impressive.

4. FUTURE REFERENCE

Once you have a disgruntled employee, you also have his pet peeve out in the open. You know precisely what's bothering him. What a bonanza! From that moment on, you can see to it that the circumstances that produced his gripe are never allowed to build up again. Given enough valid gripes, a dedicated manager ought to be able to turn himself into the perfect boss—so sensitive to employees' needs that he knows them almost before they do. An executive that good will find the gripes few and far between.

Chapter Twelve

How to Handle the Problem Employee

The problem employee need not be anyone with so deep and dramatic a problem as alcoholism, compulsive gambling or a history of chronic absenteeism, although such people certainly qualify. For purposes of this discussion, the problem employee is simply anyone whose contribution to your organization is consistently disappointing. You expect him to do one thing, but he does another. Faulty communications? Not necessarily. A businessman—any businessman—may enjoy excellent communications and still have several problem employees.

Why?

WHAT MAKES PROBLEM EMPLOYEES?

An employee may turn into a problem for any of several reasons. Among them are:

1. Lack of skill in the job
2. Misplacement
3. Lack of job structure
4. Incompatibility between employee and employer
5. Inadequate supervision

6. Emotional immaturity
7. Poor health

Or he may be a problem because his personal adjustment is poor, he feels insecure about his job or he's bothered by off-the-job difficulties.

Let's examine these possibilities in some detail.

LACK OF SKILL

Sometimes a person is a problem employee because he lacks job competence. His skill may have been sufficient when you hired him, but—for one reason or another—it hasn't kept pace with the demands of the job. This inability to perform his job as well as he would like, or as well as he thinks you expect him to, can adversely affect an employee in a number of ways. It can, for example, make him sullen and uncooperative with his fellow workers. It can cause frictions in his relationships with his own family which, by adding to his emotional burdens, reinforce the pattern of poor performance on the job, thus setting up a vicious circle, frustration feeding on frustration. It can even trigger a series of psychological crises for him by lowering his self-esteem.

MISPLACEMENT

Sometimes an employee becomes a problem because he is in the wrong job. Perhaps he is selling and failing miserably because he lacks self-confidence. He begins to suspect that customers don't like him. In some cases, this feeling causes him to act in a hostile manner toward them, adding further to his lack of success.

LACK OF JOB STRUCTURE

Without detailed and clear instructions in what they are to do or a precise definition of their responsibilities, most employees become confused. When an employee wonders why he doesn't know his job, he may decide, "It's my fault. I didn't pay enough attention when the boss was explaining it." Or more likely, he will blame his employer: "That so-and-so never says what he wants and then jumps on me when I do it wrong." Either conclusion damages his ego—and morale.

INCOMPATIBILITY

Some people are problems because of simple incompatibility between them and their bosses. "I just can't get along with him," a production line worker says about his supervisor. And the supervisor says, "No matter how hard I try to understand him and make allowances, he rubs me the wrong way." What causes such friction between two people, both of whom are trying to cooperate? Some call it "personality clash" or "bad chemistry." Actually, it is far more complicated than these labels imply. The important point is: be aware of such incompatibility and realize that, until we learn a great deal more than we now know about what makes the human psyche tick, there isn't very much you can do to change it.

INADEQUATE SUPERVISION

Employees frequently become problems because of inadequate supervision. In some cases, they don't know what to do and the boss doesn't seem to care when or how they do it. People begin to deteriorate when they aren't kept busy at constructive tasks. They lose interest, grow indifferent and sometimes resentful. Closely related to this situation is inconsistent or capricious supervision. One day the boss is strict; the next day he's lax. Employees don't know what to expect from him. "Some days he treats me awful," one employee says, "but on other days he lets me get away with murder."

EMOTIONAL IMMATURITY

Other employees are problems because they never grew up emotionally. Frequently, they think and act like children. They see "plots" against themselves; they sulk; they are super-sensitive and easily offended. To a certain extent everyone suffers from this condition. The difference between an emotionally immature person and one who is normal is that the normal person has *fewer* emotional disturbances. And he is better able to control them than his more volatile colleague.

POOR HEALTH

The human body changes constantly. Deterioration sets in early with some people, later with others, but eventually with everyone. Sometimes it's sudden, as when an apparently healthy person suffers a heart attack. Or it may be gradual, as when an employee loses his hearing over a period of years. Often, the most difficult problems created by such poor health conditions are the anxiety and psychological damages that accompany changing physical conditions. For example, nature may repair an employee's damaged heart so that he's almost as good as new, but he may never overcome his anxiety. His constant fear of another attack may turn him into a whining or cantankerous problem employee.

WHAT CAN YOU DO?

Even though handling problem employees is a complex management problem, there are things you can do to help yourself and your employees. First of all, try not to hire problem people or ones who seem to be potential problems.

But how do you spot trouble-in-the-making? In at least three ways.

1. HAVE CLEAR-CUT EMPLOYMENT SPECIFICATIONS

Two conditions are necessary here. First, you need to know the details of the job in question. Second, you must know what sort of person can best fill the job.

Suppose you need a stock clerk. Make a list of the elements

in his job so you will know the number of different things the employee has to do. Estimate as accurately as you can the amount of time each task takes in an average day. This is an important key to what kind of person to hire. For example, if the person is to spend six hours a day arranging and dusting stock and two hours waiting on customers, you'll need a different type of employee than if the job calls for six hours of selling and two hours of stock work.

After you know what the job consists of, both in tasks and time, you can determine the sort of person you need to hire. Make a list of the characteristics he or she has to have in order to do the job: age, temperament, special skills, experience, education and the like.

For instance, if you were looking for a man to drive a fuel oil truck, the first requirement, of course, would be the ability to drive a truck. Then, he'd need the proper operator's license, a sense of responsibility, good health, the ability to keep simple records and so on.

Once you have clear-cut employment specifications in front of you, you have a far better chance of successfully matching a job applicant against job requirements than if you relied solely on chance in making your choice.

2. CHECK FORMER EMPLOYMENT

This common practice in personnel selection can be helpful in matching an applicant against your job specifications. For example, his former employers can tell you if the applicant has in any way misrepresented his qualifications.

Get the most from this device by asking *specific* questions. Hiring a typist? Ask questions such as: how long did it take her to do a one-page letter? What kind of mistakes did she make? Did she "catch on" fast? Did her previous boss delegate the writing of routine correspondence to her? Answers to such specific questions can give you facts which you can use in judging whether the applicant and the job jibe.

3. USE TESTS

Some managers short-change themselves when deciding on whether applicants meet their specifications. These men base their judgments on what they learn from interviewing applicants and from checking their former employment. However, they fail to use a third obvious tool which can give them additional decision-making material: tests.

Tests are scientific selection devices which, properly used, can help you learn a great deal about an applicant in a fairly short time. Using this information can often mean the difference between making a first-rate judgment or a borderline one.

What kind of tests and how many you use depends on the skills and personal characteristics you expect applicants to have. Most large companies have their own test programs. If yours does not, one possible source of information about available tests for your line of business or industry is your trade association.

By testing job applicants, interviewing them and checking with their former employer, you gain facts and insights which should help you to judge whether an applicant has the requisite qualifications.

Often such facts and insights can also help you spot in advance a potential problem employee. The important point is that you recognize him while you still have the option of not hiring him.

HANDLING PRESENT PROBLEMS

Sometimes businessmen are so pleased with the success they have in keeping out potential problem employees that they feel, "If only I could start over without the problem employees I hired years ago." Perhaps it's just as well that they can't. After all, an employer has certain obligations to his people as well as to his firm.

How do you blend these two obligations when dealing with problem employees?

You do it by:

1. Appraising the employee
2. Letting him know where he stands
3. Detecting problem employees early
4. Maintaining proper discipline
5. Revamping his job

APPRAISING THE EMPLOYEE

When you appraise an employee, you compare his performance with what the job requires of him. To get an accurate appraisal, one that is fair both to you and to him, you need a clear-cut description of the job and a clear-cut description of the employee's performance.

Your appraisal should be based on sound techniques and it should be periodic. Here again, your trade association may be a good source of information on appraisal systems for your type of business or industry.

LETTING THE EMPLOYEE KNOW WHERE HE STANDS

However, in order to correct the employee you have to go one step further and let him know where he stands. Sometimes, just knowing that he's headed for trouble helps a worker to improve. But don't count on it. Whenever possible, suggest specific things he or she can do.

For instance, if your appraisal shows an employee is coming in late several mornings a week, let him know that you'll be looking for this item on your next appraisal.

In the process of looking for trouble, however, don't neglect satisfactory employees. Praise them for good performances and try to help them grow. Give them at least one specific thing to do to increase their competence further. When they've mastered it, give them another. And another. And another.

DETECTING PROBLEM EMPLOYEES EARLY

Your appraisal helps you here, naturally, but it may not always detect a problem employee in the early stages. Suppose that shortly after your appraisal discussion, the employee begins to do something that may turn him into a problem. You may not be fully aware of this trend until the next appraisal time—one, two or six months later. By then the situation may be acute.

If you supervise your own people, you'll want to be alert for day-to-day changes that might indicate trouble. However, if others do all, or most, of the supervising, then your task is more complicated.

Here you'll need to do at least three things: (1) be sure your assistants understand how to deal with problem employees; (2) insist that they be alert to signs of trouble; and (3) instruct them to do whatever is necessary to help the employee correct his weaknesses.

Some people don't work out regardless of what you do to correct them. So when it's obvious that an employee is a misfit, discharge him as soon as possible. Passing him from manager to manager in the hope that he'll make the grade is unfair to both of you.

MAINTAINING PROPER DISCIPLINE

What is proper discipline? To a great extent, the answer depends on your situation. However, remember that one of the paradoxes of management is this: most employees are usually happier and more comfortable in a well-structured environment than in one that operates with disorder and permissiveness.

For most people like order. They want freedom of action, of course, but within a recognizable framework. That is, they like to know what is expected of them and they want to be able to respect their manager. Often, they feel better when he makes the decisions and takes the blame for the wrong ones.

In many cases, such proper discipline helps to correct employees who are already problems. It also tends to prevent satisfactory employees from becoming problems.

REVAMPING THE EMPLOYEE'S JOB

There are cases where the only way to correct a problem employee is to restructure his job.

For example, he and your assistant are incompatible. Both are good men, but they cannot get along together. Here you revamp the job so that the employee no longer works for the same boss.

Suppose you are the boss with only three or four employees. How do you alter a person's job when you and he cannot get along? It's not easy, but perhaps you can rearrange his schedule or his responsibilities so that your contacts with him are minimal. If you do, be sure that he understands why. He will appreciate what you are trying to do.

In other cases, you may need to change a satisfactory employee's job in some way. For instance, your secretary suddenly has to get her child off to school each morning; consequently, she cannot get to work on time. Changing her job so that she can start later in the morning and work longer in the afternoon helps her. Now she can handle her home responsibility without neglecting her work.

Remember—people do make mistakes. But try to compensate for human error by making your systems for doing things as perfect as you can.

You will never achieve perfection, to be sure. Nevertheless, it is a most desirable goal because it keeps you working toward a more efficient operation. And even more important, pursuing this goal should lead you toward more orderly procedures which make for a smoother-working, happier place of business.

There is another kind of problem employee whose needs we have not yet touched upon. His "problem" is that he is good. But if his abilities go unrecognized and unrewarded, he is apt to grow discouraged and either stop trying or move into greener pastures. Either way, you lose his potential. Because it's a loss you can ill afford to sustain, we now turn our attention to identifying these special "problem people."

Chapter Thirteen

How to Spot
and Groom a "Comer"

There are at least three good reasons why you should be on the lookout for subordinates who are ready, or approaching readiness, for promotion.

First, it is an important part of your job. Certainly, a manager's chief responsibility is to see that the things that need doing get done with dispatch by those under him. But almost as important is the development of his people for bigger opportunities. Not only does this make for good morale among employees, who obviously will be motivated by such a policy to do their best, but it is also in the best interests of your company.

Second, by making it possible for every man to realize his own highest potential and, consequently, for your firm to get the most out of the manpower at its disposal, you are making an important contribution to overall company efficiency and productivity.

Finally, by spotting the people who may one day qualify for your own job, you are insuring your own upward mobility. More than one man has frozen himself into his job by shortsightedly neglecting to groom his own successor.

Before you can bring your people along, however, you must identify those who are most ready for further development. Obviously, specific qualifications will vary from department to department. Yet, there are certain general characteristics that winners everywhere tend to share.

In seeking out the "comers" under you, look for these traits:

COMPETITIVENESS

Good executives—as well as good potential ones—cannot bear to lose at anything. They are interested only in winning. Toward that end, they are constantly evaluating themselves against the competition and striving to do better at every opportunity. One top man, of the classic self-made mold, recalls that when he was on the way up, he thought: "Here I am, swimming in an ocean filled with whales and I'm just a minnow. They might kill me, just by accident, with a yawn, because I'm a minnow and they are whales." His wife asked him, "What are you going to do about them?" His reply was, "I'm going to become a whale, too." And he did. It is this spirit, basically, that the typical "comer" evidences, even if he does not express it quite so colorfully.

DEDICATION

Dedication consists of such sub-traits as ambition, ability to work hard and a ready acceptance of responsibility. To test for this quality in a man you think may possess it, give him a project that you have been holding to handle personally and see what he does with it, how he comes through. Does he take it from you with zest and confidence? Many people are timid about assuming responsibility and few actually reach for it. When you give a man a project, watch for signs indicating that he sees beyond his immediate task and is willing to do more than is minimally required to get the job done. If you spot the signs, you have a plus reacher and, more than likely, a plus performer.

HONESTY

How honest is he with himself? Is he aware of his own limitations, as well as of his strengths? How honest is he with you?

How consistently does he produce what he says he will produce? Is his level of aspiration unrealistic or is it close to what he can actually achieve? If he says, "OK, I didn't do too well that time, but I learned a lesson and I'll do better next time around," then he's honest with himself.

MATURITY

The kind of man you are interested in knows that his own future depends on what happens to other people. He respects differences of opinion. He doesn't meddle in office politics and he refuses to use others for his own ends. He is patient. He doesn't accept the first solution when it presents itself. And he bounces back when he's hurt, tougher and wiser for having weathered the storm.

INGENUITY

Ideally, he is slightly dissatisfied with the *status quo.* He sees procedures and policies through fresh eyes and has ideas on how they can be improved. He may even be impatient with the rules under which he operates. It is, of course, unrealistic to expect him to appreciate all the ramifications and interdependencies that restrict the adoption of certain innovations. With seasoning, he will learn. Certainly, given the choice between a man who unquestioningly accepts Things-As-They-Are and a man who chafes under Standard Operating Procedures, the chafer is your better bet—providing he is not merely a chronic whiner. The comer, in short, is almost always a slightly dissatisfied man who will spot a problem that others have ignored, seek out solutions, fight for the one he thinks is best. Find a man like that and you are well on the way to having spotted a comer.

ABILITY TO LEARN

High-potential people are invariably "quick studies." They soak up information, rapidly grasp the big picture, have agile minds, relish intellectual challenge. When you talk with them, they are alert to your every word and have questions which indicate that they are thinking ahead of your immediate subject. If your answers to their questions are unsatisfactory, they will let you know. They are not the easiest people in the world to lead precisely because they are bright, but in turn you, yourself, will be kept on your toes and learn.

COMMUNICATIVENESS

If it is true that they are critical listeners, it is equally true that comers express themselves easily and effectively. They are sensitive to shades of meaning and have a respect for words, both spoken and written. Since the aim of effective communications is to reach the *mind* of another person, they select words suited to that person's level of intelligence, background and experience. If the nature of their communications requires the use of jargon, they make sure that their audience understands the specialized meanings attached to their words. They define their terms, are brief without being cryptic, avoid abstractions whenever possible. And since words are the tools of thought, they tend to be clear, straight thinkers as well. These, of course, are important qualities in men who one day may be managers themselves.

ABILITY TO GET ALONG WITH OTHERS

The man who is ready for bigger things must necessarily be capable of working with others. He cannot be a prima donna or a loner. The business world being what it is, most big jobs require the efforts of many people of diverse talents. Specific characteristics required include the ability to take criticism and criticize others with tact, help those who need it and ask for help when needed and submerge one's own ego into the general effort. Does your man possess them?

FLEXIBILITY

With changing needs taking place almost daily in every growing organization, it is essential that a comer have the necessary flexibility of mind to adjust his thinking and abilities quickly to meet needs that may be far from his immediate interests. You should see in him one who can suddenly "reverse his field" to work closely with new associates on new problems.

TIME CONSCIOUSNESS

The man with a future has a healthy respect for the time at his disposal to get things done. He is organized, has devised routine ways to dispose of routine chores and almost never misses a deadline. If he finds himself temporarily stymied on a job, he doesn't bang his head against a stone wall; instead, he has a standby chore to which he can apply his energies, returning to the tougher job refreshed and without panic.

He knows his own capabilities and can give realistic estimates of the time he will require to do whatever assignment comes his way. He has also learned the secret of pacing himself, alternating the tough with the less taxing jobs. And, in emergencies, he can—for limited periods of time—work hard and intensively.

DECISIVENESS

He has faith in his judgment and is willing to assume the responsibility for his assessment of the facts in any given situation. This is not to be confused with stubbornness—that is, the inability to admit an error. But a man marked for advancement gets as many facts bearing on a situation as he can, then does not flinch at the moment of truth: the time when he must finally weigh them and draw a conclusion, all by himself.

SELF-CONFIDENCE

The man with a future has a realistic sense of his own capabilities—what he can do and what he cannot do. He is no braggart, but at the same time he is not falsely modest. There is a middle ground, upon which his feet are firmly planted—self-confidence. He does not fear an assignment that is different from anything he may have done before, so long as it falls within the range of his abilities. Rather, he views it as an additional avenue to growth Nor does he panic under pressure. On those occasions when he fails, he does not resort to excuses and buck-passing, but freely admits that he goofed, learning something in the process.

RESOURCEFULNESS

If he needs information, he knows where to get it. If he needs help, he knows who can give it. He has, over a period of time, developed his own legitimate shortcuts to getting a job done. As a result of his know-how, in all likelihood he requires minimal supervision; he receives an assignment, then does it in a competent, often superior, way. If you have such a man, treasure him. He's a "comer."

These are the raw qualifications for a "comer." But spotting him is only half the job; you must train him, too.

Are the men who will someday replace you as you yourself move up the executive ladder or retire prepared to do so? Do they have the knowledge, ability and practical experience upon which sound decisions and growth are based? Or are you neglecting their training, unconsciously assuming that you will always be there to help and advise them?

If, upon thinking it over, you find that they could use a *lot* more training, you have probably been falling into one or more of the following management traps:

1. You are not taking into consideration the probability that your firm or department will grow and, in the future, require more knowledgeable executives.
2. You are not anticipating the need for out-thinking and out-performing your competitors.
3. If you are top man, you believe that you are immortal.

In a nutshell, there you have three excellent reasons for immediately setting up a training program for your juniors.

Can't afford it? No time? Insufficient personnel?

Not so. The truth is, you can't afford the luxury of *not* having an executive training program. And it needn't be expensive, either. The following are ten tested techniques that you can use right in the office.

DAY-TO-DAY COACHING

In training, nothing takes the place of constant observation, suggestions, and guidance on the job. Here is the one job that top brass should never delegate, for administration is the coaching of good men to make them better. The "how" of coaching is not so clearly defined as other teaching methods. It is surrounded by intangibles because, for one thing, the "how" depends on the personality of the coach; for another, coaching at the executive-trainee level varies considerably with the individual "apprentice."

Underlying all good tactics, however, is the same principle that prompts a football coach to show his varsity team movies of its scrimmages: help a man to see for himself where to improve.

The vice president in charge of production for a medium-size manufacturing company, for example, was having trouble with a junior executive and one of his foremen. He considered both men worthy of further development and eventual heavy management responsibility. Each, though, repeatedly reported how the other hampered his work. Tolerance, the president decided—that essential trait of a top man—was missing in their relationship.

He went into one of his coaching moves. He ordered the men to switch jobs for a time, explaining that a fresh approach would iron out their difficulties. The young men not only improved operations; each also gained a new understanding of the other's headaches, which erased the personal animosity between them. Indirectly they had been tactfully coached on individual weaknesses—unfriendliness and noncooperation.

Areas where daily coaching is particularly helpful include:

1. Discussions of individual strengths and weaknesses with subordinates.

2. Reduction in the internal tensions that normal, nonneurotic trainees feel. They must learn to stop pressing and, like the professional athlete, to lean into their new responsibilities, not rush into them.

3. Demonstrations of the value of creative thinking; and overcoming their secret fear that they are not accomplishing enough now that the results of their work no longer are as tangible as when they started out at lower job levels.

"MULTIPLE" MANAGEMENT

This is a training technique that passes under an assortment of names—Management Cabinets, Management Round Tables and Junior Boards of Directors.

Easily adaptable to the smaller outfit's operation, it is a way to let junior executives practice senior-executive thinking on company problems, yet leaves the final responsibility, authority and decision to top management, where it belongs.

Here is one form of operation:

Five men, say, are chosen from 15 eligibles to serve on a Junior Board of Directors. They meet every two or four weeks to discuss overall and departmental problems. They tackle specific problems and report concrete solutions to top company officers for consideration. Men serving on the Junior Board rotate over a given period of time.

At one company, the nine men who serve on the Board rate each other every six months on how well they tackle problems with a top-brass approach. The four men with the lowest ratings are dropped and four new ones from the group of eligibles replace them. Thus, every eligible junior executive participates on the Board within a 24- to 30-month period. No stigma is attached to a man who has been dropped and he can always be reappointed.

At this company, the men discuss production, engineering, and marketing problems. Recommendations, if approved by two-thirds of the board, are forwarded to the Senior Board of Directors.

"LISTENING IN"

In the case of the very small firm, or where only one or two men are in training, the closer the trainee is to the superior, the better. The physical situation is important here. The trainee should be in the same office, or readily available, so he can unobtrusively and conveniently listen to what goes on and learn from business conversations or conferences. He is like the understudy of a star performer in a play. This type of trainee could be made an "Assistant to _____."

JACK-OF-ALL-TRADES

In formal large-scale program training, one technique is labeled "job rotation." It is learning by doing a variety of jobs around headquarters, in the plant and in branch offices. Many large companies have job rotation worked out on a systematic, timetable basis.

Actually, job rotation is unconsciously practiced in smaller firms, simply because there an executive is expected to double on duties and, with a limited staff, be several men rolled into one. The point is, be sure you capitalize on the training possibilities in this situation so natural to the small business. Help the junior to see the relationship of the varied work he performs to future overall management action and knowledge.

THE CORNER LIBRARY

A bookcase in one corner of the office, kept well stocked with up-to-date material on personnel, marketing, economics, management trends, competitive company news and so forth is an effective, inexpensive training tool.

To guarantee that the material will be dog-eared, keep changing the contents of the shelves, suggest that so-and-so will find this or that helpful reading; use the books as references during group meetings. Near the bookcase, hang a bulletin board and place a magazine and newspaper rack. On the board put the latest technical bulletins, clipped news items, and mag-

azine articles of special interest; in the rack place good management magazines and business newspapers.

One word of warning: unless the contents of your bulletin
board and racks are changed periodically, people will soon lose
the habit of dropping by to read them.

GROUP MEETINGS

These can be held over coffee, during a certain hour of the
work week or after hours. They must revolve around a plan,
though, and that plan must be maintained. They should also be
under the guidance of an effective leader who can draw out
their thinking.

Such meetings can be the instrument of a series of discussions; for example, the scientific approach to management problems, what encourages high morale and cooperation among employees, the most pressing problem currently facing the department or firm.

Group meetings are also the place for trainees to practice
public speaking, counseling and advising subordinates, getting
ideas and instructions across clearly to another person.

It is not enough to discuss the principles and merits of good
public speaking or advising subordinates, training experts find.
To gain confidence and automatically react correctly, men need
practice. So, at the meetings, trainees should take turns playing
the roles of an executive and a subordinate. The "subordinate"
will interrupt, ask questions, get mad or whatever the occasion
seems to call for, according to the way the "executive" handles
the matter.

Others in the group quietly watch and listen. At the end of
the "act," they offer suggestions, criticize constructively.

FILMS

Slides and moving pictures are excellent training devices,
too. The small company can write to larger firms (which produce their own training films) for appropriate movies, borrow-
ing them for nothing or renting them at nominal fees.

VISITING SPEAKERS

Ask the head of the local Chamber of Commerce, a president from another company, a professor from a nearby college or the community's "visiting firemen" to come and talk to your trainees.

If the group is so small that complete informality is the rule, have lunch sent in and let everyone sit around a conference table eating and listening. Above all, whether a lecture or a luncheon session, allow time for a question-and-answer period.

SPECIAL ASSIGNMENTS

The special asignment can be used as a test; it is also a tool to teach delegation of authority. One manager had a very capable young man on his hands—so good that he wanted to do everything, even though he had two smart men to help him.

The manager gave him a special assignment that took him several months and overloaded him to the point where he had no time to watch every move of the other two men. When the task was finished, he was smart enough to note that these men had gotten along very well without him. He had had a good lesson in delegation.

In such cases, however, the assignment must be big enough and sufficiently interesting to absorb the man, so he will let go of other details.

OUTSIDE ASSIGNMENTS

Company work which involves getting things done through people who are *not* employees of the firm teaches the junior executive much about human relations.

Take the case of the good, but too-tough man who seemed ruthless in his attitude toward employees. His superior wondered if he could never be coached in tolerance. Except for this bad trait, the man was promising in every respect.

Finally, the superior and the firm's president decided to use their influence to have the man put in charge of a community project which was also part of a public relations problem faced by the company. In this position, in order to get work done through "civilians" who were not answerable to him as employees, the man started to develop tact, sympathy, and an ability to handle people as individuals.

Clearly, there *are* effective, inexpensive ways to get your promising subordinates prepared for bigger things, providing you yourself are big enough and wise enough to realize that no one man can hold all the reins forever and that the future belongs to those who prepare for it.

One of the criteria of your own ability as a manager is the number of people who, in a sense, "graduate" under your leadership. If you are doing your job totally and with dedication, there is a gratifying kind of turnover in your department—men leaving for bigger and better jobs within your company. Such a record marks you as a "comer" yourself. The above suggestions, used in conjunction with good judgment, should help you get where you're going a bit faster than the man who ignores or hoards his winners.

Chapter Fourteen

How to Develop a Top Assistant

Ralph Brown works for a Midwest steel fabricator and with the approval of his boss, he's taking the lead in a local Community Chest drive.

In the Southwest, Sam Brady, assistant to an oil distributor, attends a three-day management institute. It is co-sponsored by the state oil jobber association and local educators.

George Hayes, assistant manager of a store on the west coast, and his boss set aside time each week to discuss decisions which his boss made during the previous five days.

On the east coast, Sam Stern is asked to solve problems similar to those his employer faces each day, while operating an electronic testing equipment firm.

In the Southeast, Martin Wileman, a paper salesman, takes an active part in a management seminar which a large supplier holds for paper distributors.

Five men, five different jobs . . . but all have one thing in common. In each case, their boss is developing an assistant.

At some point, as you yourself scale the corporate ladder, you will find that you need a good right arm, too. In all likelihood, he will come from the ranks of promising young men you identify and train on your own way up.

Choosing and developing a top assistant is a vital business activity for several reasons. First, you gain hours weekly for other managerial duties because a good assistant can take part of your work load off your shoulders. Second, you develop a man who can step into your shoes in case of an accident to you, or an illness or a needed vacation. Third, you are adding to your firm's pool of executive talent.

CHOOSING THE ASSISTANT

The first step in developing a top assistant is making the decision to do so. Some men have trouble here because it isn't easy for them to relax their grip on the reins of responsibility. Any mistake the assistant makes reflects on them.

The actual choice of assistant is another major step. How, after all, do you know you are getting the right person?

If the man is to be promoted from within, you have had an opportunity to observe him over a period of time. You can test him by giving him some management assignments prior to his promotion. If you tap your assistant from the outside, give him a thorough interview. Check his references and talk with his former employers.

One important suggestion: even though your assistant must have the same abilities as you, try to find a man who complements rather than mirrors you. Strangely enough, two dynamic and aggressive individuals are apt to set sparks flying in a short time. The capable assistant is most often one whose strengths match your weaknesses rather than one whose strong points match yours.

QUALITIES TO LOOK FOR

You cannot expect to find a well-rounded manager who is ready and willing to move in to help you. You'll have to train and work with him.

You need a man who will profit from your experience. He should be the type of person who wants to and *can* learn fast. He should be able to think and have common sense. He must possess the ability to work with people and gain their confidence. And he must be able to lead because he will become "you" to your subordinates and colleagues.

If he has these qualities plus initiative, you can teach him to handle additional responsibility and authority. He can learn the skills of management, such as planning and supervising the work of others.

You might, for example, assign him the management task of hiring new employees. Learning such work will increase his understanding of the various phases of your business or department. The more he learns about it, the greater will be his satisfaction with his job. A good assistant will thrive on responsibility and a varied work routine.

HOW TO DELEGATE RESPONSIBILITY

In order to develop an assistant so that he can do his best, you will have to work closely with him. In addition to personal guidance, you should lay a solid foundation for your assistant's spot in your firm.

The following suggestions can be helpful:

GIVE HIM THE FACTS

See that your assistant has all the necessary facts about his new responsibility. Give him a clear picture of what he is to do and how he should do it. Tell him how much responsibility and authority he is to have. One way to start is by helping him develop a description of his new job. Tell him whom he will be working with and personally introduce him to these people. Make certain they understand that they are to deal with your assistant and not with you in the future.

SMOOTH HIS PATH

Inform employees who will work with your assistant to cooperate with him. You can smooth his path by spelling out for them the areas of responsibility you've given him. Then impress on him the importance of earning the respect of other employees even when he has to reprimand them.

SHARE YOUR KNOWLEDGE

If he is to do a good job, you must keep him informed of your plans, their progress and your reasons for making each move. He should also be warned of problems that may arise. See that he learns the ins and outs of working with the other people in your firm.

ADD RESPONSIBILITY GRADUALLY

Let him get the feel of his job. By being assigned additional responsibilities in small doses, he will learn to handle new problems and, consequently, grow as a manager.

HOLD A LOOSE REIN

Some executives make the mistake of trying to keep their fingers on every move that is made in their operations. Their constant checking may make their understudies nervous and inhibit their development. Rather than cause an assistant to lose confidence in himself and his initiative, it is more advisable to hold a loose rein.

GIVE HIM AUTHORITY

Follow the management-by-exception principle when you give your assistant responsibility for a certain task. Give him the necessary authority for getting that job done and encourage him to bring problems to you only if something seems wrong or out of line. Train your assistant to give you one or more suggested solutions to the problem he brings to you. Help him develop by guiding him to make the correct decision.

HOW MUCH CONTROL FOR YOU?

When you delegate authority and responsibility to an assistant, you are using his ability to think, plan, act and evaluate. Of course, you have to stay in the driver's seat. Control is important so that you can blend his progress in with the overall activities for which you are responsible.

Check regularly on assignments which you give your assistant. But don't subject every little detail to microscopic examination.

Some advice here. Your assistant probably will not do the job in precisely the same way you would. His approach may be as different from yours as his handwriting is different. It may even be better. So long as he gets the results you want, don't nag him about his methods.

WHEN HE GOOFS

Everyone makes mistakes and your assistant, a younger man without your experience and knowledge, will make an occasional error. Keep in mind, though, that a capable person learns from mistakes.

If you need to correct your assistant on a specific project, do it in private. On the other hand, praise him in public. In private, discuss calmly the mistake and point out how he can avoid the error in the future.

TRAINING YOUR ASSISTANT

The simplest way to train your assistant is to sit down and talk with him. Explain the day-to-day running of your department or business, the problems you face, the principles of management he should know and the plans and policies of your firm.

Then turn him loose, adding management responsibilities

as fast as he can assume them. Of course, you should be available to answer questions.

Along with your discussions and his on-the-job practice in management, encourage your assistant to study and improve himself. He should read the trade publications in your line of business or industry, as well as general business papers and magazines.   ,

Your assistant should also talk to suppliers' representatives and to customers in order to learn their views and needs.

You can supplement this on-the-job training by using help from the outside to orient your assistant. Take advantage, for example, of:

COMMUNITY AND CIVIC ORGANIZATIONS

When you encourage your assistant to participate in activities such as the Junior Chamber of Commerce, a civic club or fund-raising drives, he gains experience in organizing projects. In these activities, he works without your guidance with citizens in your community. Many of them are your present or future customers.

TRADE ASSOCIATION CONFERENCES AND CONVENTIONS

Your trade association is often another source of sound training. The assistant can attend a management institute which your association holds for one to three or four days.

Many association convention programs devote part of their time to sessions on specific industry problems. In such meetings, your assistant can gain a better insight into the "big picture" of your business. He can also make contacts with men of his own level from other firms. Such contacts can give him a source of new ideas and solutions to problems which firms similar to yours have overcome.

SUPPLIER TRAINING PROGRAMS

More and more suppliers are conducting management and sales training programs for their customers and their junior executives. Frequently, such programs are conducted at the supplier's office or factory. In other cases, they may be held in the field.

HOLDING A GOOD ASSISTANT

Having developed a good assistant, your big job may become holding him. Some businessmen don't want to take the time to train an assistant adequately. Instead, they let *you* do the job for them and then try to hire your man. You can overcome this possibility by making it worthwhile for your assistant to grow along with your firm.

Right from the start, show your assistant that the job will pay off for him and his family. Let him know what his prospects are for greater financial gain. Or you may want to discuss only part of his expectations. If you withhold word of other rewards for various stages of his development, make sure that he understands that you plan to reward his efforts as your firm or department grows.

In some firms, the added responsibility that goes with being an assistant may bring him the opportunity to buy part or all of the business in the future, whether it is in the form of stock options or a junior partnership. Whether or not this is the case, the good assistant deserves a good income and has to be paid well in salary or bonus. If he isn't taken care of in one firm, often he will move on to another which does appreciate his abilities.

Developing a top assistant can pay off in a number of ways. It can make your own job easier, for example, because an assistant can give you the time to sit, plan, think and meet emergencies. And with a competent and trusted assistant, you can take time away from your business to do things with your family and friends. In effect, the proper assistant, after he is adequately trained and guided, can help you to live a fuller life both at work and at home.

✿   ✿   ✿

So we come to the end of *Managing Others Creatively*. Like all books on the subject, this one has necessarily dealt with generalities. They are valid enough so far as they go. But when it comes to applying them, you will, of course, have to use your own best judgment in terms of your particular situation and your particular people.

People! Male, female, young, old, ambitious, lazy, dedicated, sensitive, independent, brilliant, dull, cooperative, stubborn, contradictory, spiteful, unpredictable, infuriating people! Like snowflakes, no two are alike.

Yet people are your chief raw material. You are expected to understand them, train them, inspire them, lead them, somehow work with—and through—them. There is probably no tougher job in the business world. And if you read one hundred —or one hundred times one hundred—books on the art of managing others, you would still not have all the answers, for not only is every individual unique, but the interaction between any two people represents an equation never before expressed. Add a third person and you complicate that equation still further. Add a fourth, fifth, sixth or more and you soon have a unique amalgam of psyches, needs, motives and points of view that, for sheer quantity and subtlety, stagger the mind.

That's what makes managing people so fascinating, so challenging and, when done successfully, so incomparably satisfying.